THE FRACTURED MIRROR

Healing Multiple Personality Disorder

C.W. Duncan, Ph.D.

Health Communications, Inc.
Deerfield Beach, Florida

Library of Congress Cataloging-in-Publication Data

Duncan, C. W.
      p.   cm.
Includes bibliographical references and index.
ISBN,1-55874-275-1 (pb): $9.95
1. Multiple personality — Popular works.   I. Title.
RC569.5.M8D86   1993   93-46942
616.85'236—dc20   CIP

© 1994 C.W. Duncan
ISBN 1-55874-75-1

Publisher: Health Communications, Inc.
              3201 S.W. 15th Street
              Deerfield Beach, Florida 33442-8190

Cover design by Andrea Perrine Brower

To Priscilla Cogan
wife, colleague and best friend

Gaze into a fractured mirror.
Look deeply into it, and you will see
many eyes and distorted versions of your face.
Multiple personality disorder is like a
fractured mirror, reflecting fragmented
visions of yourself. Although a broken
mirror cannot be repaired, commitment,
tenacity and hard work can bring
wholeness to your personality system.
This book will show you how.

CONTENTS

ACKNOWLEDGMENTS

The contents of this book are in large part based on the writings and lectures of those men and women who are modern pioneers in the research and treatment of dissociative disorders. My special respect to Frank Putnam, M.D., Richard Kluft, M.D., Catherine Fine, Ph.D., and Colin Ross, M.D., for their research and clinical studies in multiple personality disorder (MPD). My appreciation also is extended to John G. Watkins, Ph.D., and Helen Watkins, M.A., for their seminal work in ego states. Additionally I am indebted to Bessel van der Kolk, M.D., for his exciting study of the brain/trauma relationships.

I am very grateful for the generous way in which these clinical researchers have shared their data with rank and file therapists. They have worked tirelessly to teach mental health professionals about MPD and other dissociative disorders, and their work is reflected in every page of this book.

My appreciation includes Priscilla Cogan, Ph.D., my wife and colleague, who piqued my interest in the field of dissociation. She has also given countless hours to editing this manuscript and to helping me to clarify my presentation. Thanks also go to Sharon Johnson, who gave me the benefit of her honest feedback and editorial suggestions. Finally I am indebted to my dissociative clients, who never cease to inspire me with their courage and commitment.

INTRODUCTION

The very idea that we might have separate and discrete internal personalities strikes at our basic self-concept as whole beings. The recent public fascination with multiple personality disorder (MPD) suggests that many of us worry about the unity of our psyches. We ponder MPD with a combination of attraction and fear.

Truth is, we are all "multiple" to some degree. Thousands of participants in the Recovery Movement, for example, are discovering and nurturing their inner children. When they learn about the child personalities in MPD, many people in recovery groups worry that they too may have multiple personality disorder. Many do, but most do not. *The Fractured Mirror* can help you decide whether the MPD criteria fit, and it gives the information needed to embark upon and complete a successful therapy. Therapists who discover dissociated systems in some of their abuse-surviving clients will also find this book a valuable aid.

The Fractured Mirror is a unique book because it takes into account the richness of the total personality as expressed through the many alter selves. Multiple personality systems usually include one or more child alters who also want to know about MPD. In this book you'll find three stories to be read aloud for internal child alters, for the metaphorical nature of stories allows them to reach the whole MPD system when nothing else can. "The Princess Of The Dark Cloak" and "The Devil And Auntie" were written for some very special "children" by Dr. Priscilla Cogan, who is a clinical psychologist specializing in the treatment of dissociative disorders and MPD, and is also a novelist, poet and writer of tales. "The Legend of the Ektena" is a traditional Cherokee legend retold by the author.

Try reading each story aloud so that everyone in the system can enjoy and learn from it. Child alters usually carry the most horrendous abuse memories and must be enlisted in the therapy process. Stories such as the ones in this book will help them understand their MPD and how they can help in recovery.

The Fractured Mirror is intended for four groups of readers. First, there is the burgeoning group of people newly diagnosed or in the early phases of MPD treatment. In fact several authorities suggest dissociative disorders and MPD will be *the* diagnostic categories for the 1990s. Current research indicates that perhaps 2 percent of the general population suffers from MPD: from 5 percent to 10 percent of the mental health clinic population may be constituted of undiagnosed MPDs — thousands of people.

Second, spouses and other relatives of MPD survivors are usually puzzled and often overwhelmed by the intensity and chaos implicit in MPD. Family relationships are typically strained and may be broken by the problems brought on by multiplicity. *The Fractured Mirror* gives the rationale of treatment and illuminates the path to wholeness. Such information and the assurance that MPD can be treated and cured often means the difference between divorcing and staying together.

The third group, participants in various recovery programs, particularly ACA, ACOA, and SIA, will be interested in this material. The 35-page handbook that preceded *The Fractured Mirror*, given to MPD clients as a guide to the therapy process, was copied repeatedly and found its way through many support groups. People in recovery read widely; they are very self-aware, and many are thinking about MPD. Therefore, this book is ideal for them.

Finally, more and more mental health professionals are now diagnosing and treating MPD. Dr. Colin Ross, one of the primary researchers in the field, writes:

> I estimate that the number of mental health professionals who made their first independent diagnosis of MPD during the 1980s in North America is between 1,000 and 5,000. Counting ward nursing staff, nonmedical therapists, psychiatry residents on call, community-based counselors and all other mental health professionals, I estimate that as many as 10,000 professionals have had direct contact with diagnosed MPD cases in North America during the last ten years. I am referring only to professionals who considered the diagnosis to be legitimate and correct.

The Fractured Mirror is brief, concise, accurate and to the point. Mental health professionals and students will find it a useful aid in the treatment of dissociation and MPD, although it is only a starting point. Professionals will need to study the more technical books on MPD and avail themselves of special training in the diagnosis and treatment of all dissociative disorders.

The main goal of this book is to remove MPD from the realm of the bizarre and strange and place it firmly in the realm of normal defenses that have gone awry. People with multiple personality disorder suffer from internal chaos, roller-coaster emotions and terrible memories. They present confusing and contradictory images to their families and friends. In spite of all that, MPD is an eminently treatable disorder. Unlike bipolar affective disorders or the psychoses, multiple personality disorder can be overcome so that the MPD label is no longer applicable.

There is no substitute for a competent psychotherapist, but this book is an excellent road map. It suggests ways in which people with MPD can facilitate their own therapy, and it should help family and friends understand and support the process.

You need not read this book in any specific order. If you are newly diagnosed with MPD, you might want to read Chapter 6, on therapy and therapists, first.

MPD affects both men and women, although women are much more likely to be in treatment than are men. To eliminate the awkwardness of he/she and similar devices, please understand that when I speak of an MPD client (or therapist) as male or female, I am including both sexes.

ONE

The Story Of MPD

The story of multiple personalties and dissociation is as ancient as the human race. Although this book is intended to help you understand *your* MPD — your symptomatology, your therapy, your prognosis and your potential problems — it must begin with the rich and fascinating history of MPD.

As you ponder this history, notice an arresting bit of synchronicity: the narrative is replete with examples of dissociation. There is the dissociation of Freudian psychiatry from any consideration of trauma-based behavioral patterns. There is the dissociation of behavioral psychology and biological (medication-oriented) psychiatry from concern with internal psychological processes. Even within the overall field of dissociation, there are groups so dissociated from one another that they appear to be unaware of, and certainly unaffected by, their respective contributions: for instance, until recently few publications on MPD mention the seminal work by John Watkins on ego states. Dissociation is alive and active within the mental health professions!

The concept of multiplicity is at least as old as oral history. Well-known MPD researcher Colin Ross describes the Osiris myth of ancient Egypt as a metaphor for multiplicity. My own people, the Cherokee, have many legends of beings who would assume different personalities or forms as different situations demanded. In the Legend of Ektena, the warrior was transformed into a great dragon, protector of the people. He then evolved into a persecutor of the people, and finally emerged as a healing source for the Cherokee.

Even now, through sacred ceremony, native medicine people may go through transformative experiences. Often these are possession experiences in which the individual "becomes" a bear or an eagle; or a spiritual teacher may emerge from the other world through the medicine person. Eskimo and Siberian shamans have a long tradition of possession for healing and other ceremonial purposes.

These transformative possession experiences are not the same as MPD, but they are clearly dissociative processes. After all, MPD is just the radical use of dissociation in ways that were crucial for an abused child but counterproductive for an adult. If you consider dissociation and multiple-self presentations from a historical perspective, you will understand how dissociation has blessed human cultures. Perhaps you will even accept your extraordinary dissociative ability as a gift turned sour and not view it as an inherent defect in your personality.

Colin Ross suggested that the study of multiple personalities could be divided as follows:

PERIOD 1: HAZY BEGINNINGS

The story of MPD begins with the demon-possession mania of the Middle Ages, a grim time for many people. The lower classes were repressed and abused by the ruling classes and the church. We might guess that conditions were even more ripe for the production of MPD during the medieval period than they are today.

During the Middle Ages, anything unknown and frightening was attributed to religion or to the occult. Possession by demonic spirits accounted for deviant behavior. The theologian Nevius listed the following specific criteria for determining demon possession:

1. The personality says he is a demon.
2. He uses first-person pronouns for demons and third-person pronouns for the host.
3. The demon uses titles or names.
4. The demon has sentiments, facial expressions and physical manifestations that are "demonic."
5. The demon has knowledge or intellectual power not possessed by the host.
6. The demon professes hatred for God and/or Christ.

For example, when a woman began to "talk and act like a man," began to curse and be violent, it was obvious to her priest and family that she was demon-possessed. Nevius's list holds many characteristics of alters that I have met in my practice. If you have MPD, you may very well recognize these criteria in yourself.

It is also interesting to note that Satanism and the Black Mass came from the medieval period. The ruling classes, including the church, had become intolerably oppressive. The church attempted to eliminate the Dionysian elements of life: sensuality, spontaneity, fertility, earth religion (which the church called witchcraft) and physical ecstasy. These human characteristics could not be repressed forever; and when these characteristics combined with anger over the generally oppressive environment, some nuns, priests and laity rebelled. When these individuals broke through the repression, the Dionysian drives often took over in caricatured forms as demon possession and satanic worship. In Satanism, what the church labeled as good became evil while evil became good. Satanists worshiped everything that the church opposed. The ceremonies and sacraments of the church's mass were turned upside down in mockery. There were priests who served the church by day and Satan by night.

A few therapists and writers continue to describe certain MPD alters as "departed souls" or "demons." If these therapists are correct, it is interesting that other therapists have had success in treating these "demons" just as they treat all other alters. Ross reports that 28.6 percent of his patients believed they had demonic alters and that these alters responded very well to psychotherapy.

Warning: Having an alter claim to be a demon or demonic does not make it so. If you accept that claim at face value, you may be acquiescing to an alter who would claim demonic status as a way to protect the secrecy of traumatic memories and to thwart progress in therapy.

During the Middle Ages, the church treated demonic possession by exorcism. It is not unusual even today for certain religious denominations to engage regularly in exorcism for what they believe to be demon possession. When mental health therapists use the old technique of repressing or "hypnotizing away" alter personalities, they are attempting a psychological rather than an ecclesiastical exorcism. No research suggests that psychological exorcism is effective in dismissing difficult alters.

By the late 1600s, a dim new light began to shine on the question of multiplicity. Paracelsus, one of the early pioneers in the study of "magnetism" (hypnosis), described the first case of MPD. He described and treated, without exorcism, a female patient who had an alter personality who stole money and an amnesic host personality who knew nothing about either the theft or the alter ego state.

Through the 1700s the literature on MPD is fairly sparse. In the early 1800s, Benjamin Rush, signer of the Declaration of Independence and first Surgeon General of the Continental Army, wrote the initial American psychiatric text. He collected case histories of dissociation and multiple personalities for his lectures on physiological psychology. Rush hypothesized that the doubling of consciousness arose from a disconnection between the two hemispheres of the brain.

One of the most carefully documented cases of MPD in that period was that of Mary Reynolds, as described by

Samuel Latham Mitchell in 1811. Mary was the daughter of a Baptist minister. Although no physical or intellectual problems were noted, at the age of 18 she began to have seizures. After one serious attack, she became blind and deaf for five weeks. Although her hearing returned suddenly, she regained her sight more gradually. Later, after Mary's vision had returned to normal, she was found lying comatose in bed. When finally restored to consciousness she had no memory of her life and knew very few words. She recognized no one. She was like a newborn, but she learned quickly owing to a "mature intellect." Five weeks later she reawoke to her former self.

In her presymptomatic state she was sedate, sober and pensive. In the second and amnesic state she was light, gay and cheerful. The first state had no knowledge of the second, and the second state was amnesic about the first. She had two separate and mutually amnesic personalities. She alternated between them for 16 or 17 years and finally settled into the second personality for the final 25 years of her life.

By 1830 a very important transition was taking place. The church had always held responsibility for treating possession states through the ceremony of exorcism. As Western society moved through the Great Enlightenment during the late eighteenth and early nineteenth centuries, physicians replaced the clergy in treating these conditions. Prior to 1830 most alter personalities were identified as demonic. By 1830, severely dissociated individuals were described as being possessed not only by demons but also by the dead. Even as treatment shifted from the liturgical to the psychological arena, so its form shifted from clerical to psychological exorcism. The effect of either treatment was to drive the alters into hiding.

PERIOD 2: ESTABLISHMENT AND ELABORATION OF MPD (1880-1910)

Between 1880 and 1910, many articles were published in professional journals about dissociative phenomena, in-

cluding MPD. William James, credited by many as the father
of American psychology, discussed MPD and the plurality
of selves in his book *Principles Of Psychology*. He believed
that most human beings have several selves.

In 1902 Carl Jung, the great Swiss psychoanalyst, described possession states and dissociation in his treatise
*On The Psychology And Pathology Of So-Called Occult Phenom-
ena*. It was partially because of his interest in dissociation
that he ultimately broke with Freud and established his
own brand of analysis.

Pierre Janet, however, was the pivotal figure in the early
study of dissociation. As a young scientist, Janet studied
hypnosis and became interested in the entire process of
dissociation. Leonie, a unique patient who was a proficient
hypnotic subject, was referred to him. Janet devised a se-
ries of experiments with her, many of which formed the
basis of his theories. His studies of amnesia, fugue states,
alter personalities and other dissociative phenomena led
Janet to postulate that a personality may have split-off
parts capable of separate lives and able to affect the whole
personality and behavior. He also believed these splits were
caused by past traumatic experience. In a laboratory setting, he was able to establish the presence of a "second
self" in an MPD subject by using distraction and hypnosis
and other similar techniques. An objective researcher, he
was careful to avoid overinterpreting his observations.

It is tragic that Janet was totally eclipsed by Freudians
and behavioral psychologists, and that for so long dissociative and MPD phenomena were ignored by the American psychiatric and psychological communities. Although
he lived until 1947, Janet worked and wrote in relative
isolation from the mental health community, which was
dominated by Freud and the behaviorists. Janet's genius
remained unappreciated until modern researchers began
to discover the rich heritage he had left the field of dissociation.

By the time of his death, Janet had described virtually
everything known about dissociation today. Modern researchers have been rediscovering Janet's work, which had

been set aside when Freudian and behavioral psychology dissociated all interest in dissociation.

Morton Prince was a highly influential psychologist who published many articles on multiplicity and dissociation. His most famous MPD case history is that of "Miss Beauchamp" (a pseudonym), most notable today as a description of what treatment should *not* be.

Miss Beauchamp came to Prince as a quiet and reserved 23-year-old college student suffering from many hysterically based ailments, including headaches, insomnia and body pains. Prince soon uncovered three additional personalities: B2 was the hypnotized self, which Prince considered to be a hypnotic artifact rather than a real personality. B3 was an interesting alter who called herself Sally and claimed to have total recall. She insisted that she never slept. Sally knew all about the host personality, B1, whom she despised, and she would victimize B1 with endless practical jokes. B4 on the other hand, was an irritable and quick-tempered personality.

Prince's first objective was to determine which alter was the "real" Miss Beauchamp. He decided that while Sally was the most interesting and vital alter and certainly the one he liked most, she was not the "real" Miss Beauchamp, but merely a collective of dissociated states.

He further believed that B1 (the host) was not a real person, but a "quasi-somnambulist" (whatever that is). She would have to be "sacrificed." Therefore, Prince determined that B4 was the personality best fitted to be the real and final Miss Beauchamp.

Later, unhappy with this tack, Prince concluded that B1 and B4 should be fused into a new personality and B3 annihilated. To accomplish the annihilation, he plotted with B1 and B4 to "squeeze" Sally, B3, out of existence. Prince said, "The resurrection of the real Miss Beauchamp is through the death of Sally."

Today knowledgeable therapists would never designate a "real" personality and play God by "sacrificing" an alter. Since the whole personality is made up of all the alter parts, each must be honored and involved if the treatment process is to be successful. Unfortunately some therapists are still practicing nineteenth century therapy by trying to exorcise MPD alters rather than to heal the MPD system.

PERIOD 3: FULL MATURITY AND RAPID DECLINE OF THEORY OF MPD (1910-1980)

In the early 1900s, two very important theories began to emerge that effectively stopped clinical and laboratory research in dissociation and MPD.

The first theory, derived from Ivan Pavlov's study of conditioning and learning, led to the behavioral movement in psychology. Behaviorism accounted for human learning and conduct in terms of conditioning and reinforcement. According to this theory, we tend to increase behavior that causes pleasure and to avoid actions that cause pain. Behaviorists believed that "mind" and "spirit" were unnecessary concepts. The American school of behaviorism, which captured and dominated psychology for many years, repressed the study of dissociation and MPD as irrelevant.

The second theory came from Sigmund Freud. In 1895, Freud and his colleague Josef Breuer published their *Studies On Hysteria*. They were impressed with the hypnoid qualities of hysteria; they initially believed that hysteria was caused by the childhood trauma reported by their patients.

By 1910, however, Freud had broken with Breuer and repudiated childhood sexual trauma as the basis of hysteria. Freud wrote that reports of sexual trauma came from little girls' or women's incestuous daydreams about their fathers. As he repudiated the reality of incest, Freud also discredited hypnosis as a treatment modality, and the field of psychoanalysis eliminated dissociation and multiple personalities as a legitimate topic of study.

From 1920 to 1980, there were very few published studies of MPD. Only 14 were published from 1944 to 1969. This drop in studies of MPD stands in stark contrast to the growth of studies in psychoanalysis, which rapidly became the standard psychiatric psychotherapy.

During the 1930s schizophrenia as a diagnostic entity rose in popularity. Many biological psychiatrists eschewed the "talking therapies" and believed that all mental problems were products of brain dysfunction rather than of unresolved inner conflicts, as described by the psychoanalysts. Undoubtedly most multiples were diagnosed as schizophrenic at the time. Many still are.

Ross spoke the poignant truth when he wrote that during this period two multiples with the same symptoms might be diagnosed as a borderline or hysteric by the Freudians or as schizophrenic by the biological psychiatrists. In any case, the treatment of the MPD individual was deemed inappropriate.

The Three Faces Of Eve was the most notable account of MPD reported during the period bound by the rise of psychoanalysis in the early 1900s and the publication of *Sybil* in 1973. Eve's story did not present any new material for understanding MPD, but it did stir up much interest in what was considered a rare phenomenon. *The Three Faces Of Eve* was ultimately made into a popular movie starring Joanne Woodward.

After lengthy treatment involving several therapists, Eve came to understand that her multiplicity was a defense against painful feelings and that if she could endure the discomfort of those feelings, she would no longer need the services of alter personalities.

For many of us who received our training before the 1980s, Eve's was the only MPD case we encountered in mental health literature. I remember a very confident professor saying in 1968, "Most of Eve's personalities were caused by reinforcement from psychologists and medical interns. She enjoyed their attention. By creating more and more personalities, Eve made sure they would continue to come see her." He added, "You will probably never see an MPD case in your whole career. If, by chance, you do, ignore the alter personalities and treat only the personality that comes into your office. If you ignore the alters and refuse to credit their reality, they will go away." He was wrong!

PERIOD 4: THE RESURGENCE OF INTEREST IN MPD (1980-1984)

Historical movements usually do not begin and end on specific dates. The resurgence of interest in MPD actually began with Cornelia Wilbur's treatment of a multiple personality patient. This landmark case served as the basis for the very popular book *Sybil*, in which Wilbur was shown to be a concerned, committed and open-minded psychotherapist, treating a multiple in a caring and constructive manner without attempting to exorcise or repress the alters. The book graphically detailed her work with amnesia, fugue states, severe child abuse and conflicts among the alters. She paved the way for modern treatment approaches to dissociation and MPD. Even more important Wilbur demonstrated that multiple personality disorder could be successfully treated. The nearly universal rejection of MPD as a topic of scientific discussion was dramatically illustrated by psychiatry's refusal to publish any of Wilbur's work. After years of being ignored by her colleagues, she enlisted the help of Flora Rheta Schreiber, who wrote the story of Sybil and brought the existence of MPD into the light of popular consciousness. Only then did the mental health community begin to recognize multiple personality disorder. Today there are thousands of clients being treated for MPD and dissociation.

Three streams of influence were driving this new interest in MPD. The first stream dated from the end of World War II, when there was a resurgence in the study of hypnosis and hypnotherapy. A second push occurred during the time of the Vietnam war, which produced a flood of studies on veterans with post-traumatic stress disorder (PTSD). Politically active feminism provided the third impetus by demanding that the mental health and medical communities, law enforcement agencies and the public recognize the prevalence of incest and sexual abuse.

The first two streams provided the tools for understanding dissociation and the traumatic etiology of MPD. The third broke the conspiracy of silence around incest

and sexual abuse and forced mainstream mental health
therapists to jettison Freud's notion that incest reports
were simply the patient's incest fantasies. The stage was
set for a flowering of interest in the diagnosis and treatment of multiple personality disorder.

Finally, in 1980, MPD was included for the first time as
a diagnostic category in *The Diagnostic and Statistical Manual
III*. This inclusion officially established MPD's diagnostic
legitimacy.

PERIOD 5: MODERN SCIENTIFIC STUDY
OF MPD (1984-PRESENT)

The "modern era" of the scientific study of dissociation
and MPD can be dated from October 1983 when a special
issue of *The Journal Of Clinical Hypnosis* was devoted entirely
to MPD. The following year three psychiatric journals —
The International Journal Of Clinical And Experimental Hypnosis,
The Psychiatric Annals and *Psychiatric Clinics Of North America*
— published special issues on dissociation and MPD.

In 1984 the First International Conference on Multiple
Personality/Dissociative States was held in Chicago. The
International Society for the Study of Multiple Personality
and Dissociation (ISSMP&D) was founded in the same
year. The ISSMP&D journal, *Dissociation*, followed in
1988. For the first time in the modern era, scholarly books
on multiple personality and dissociation were being published. It was an exciting time for practitioners in the field
of dissociation and MPD.

With the growing number of case studies and research
reports and the establishment of an international society,
the field of dissociation finally achieved the political power
and scientific clout necessary to make a lasting impact on
psychiatry and psychology.

Colin Ross summed it up well:

> These developments in the last half decade make it un-
> likely that MPD will once again fall into oblivion after a
> short period of enthusiasm. The field is creating a data
> base that should bring it into the psychiatric mainstream.

One of the most important events in this regard was the launching of the journal *Dissociation* in 1988. With a professional society, a journal, a major specialty meeting, a number of scholarly books, and papers in a variety of journals, the dissociative disorders have begun to establish themselves in psychiatry, as the anxiety disorders did only a short while ago. There are many patients with treatable dissociative disorders in North America who could benefit from greater awareness, prompter diagnosis, and more skilled treatment than is often available to them.

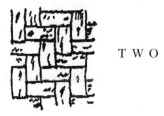

T W O

Multiple Personality Disorder: An Overview

You have been tentatively diagnosed as having MPD. You knew you were moody and changeable. Family and friends may have complained, "You are never the same way twice." They laughed and called you a Gemini. You laughed too, a bit uncomfortably, no doubt. One of your friends in the incest survivors group has MPD, but it has never occurred to you that you might have it too. Or has it? Maybe you thought, "Possibly," but quickly dismissed it as unlikely. Oh, you had heard about multiple personality disorder from books, movies, TV soaps and talk shows, but you thought, "Surely, I am not like them," and you buried the hunch deep inside.

"The doctor said that I may have MPD." "No, I don't!" "Yes, I do!" "That's ridiculous!" "No, it isn't!" The internal argument continued, but the question hovered in the air like a stubborn mosquito.

You need answers fast, something that will quell the storm inside, something you can hang on to, some facts about this "strange malady." This book will give you facts, the good and the bad, so that you can judge for yourself whether or not you have MPD. If you come to accept your tentative diagnosis, this book will help you prepare for successful therapy. No other psychotherapy requires so much of your intelligent cooperation as does MPD therapy, and no psychotherapy promises so successful an outcome, if you truly commit yourself to it.

MPD is a dissociative disorder, an excessive use of the mind's natural ability to lose itself in daydreaming, visualizing and creating. Dissociation is a normal, everyday human activity. You are dissociated, for example, when you lose track of time while reading a novel or when you are driving and lost in thought. The writer who is "dreaming" a story line and unaware of her surroundings is dissociated. Everyone dissociates. It is a great escape from tedium. But if dissociation fills so much of your time that it interferes with your work or the quality of your life, it has become a problem rather than a useful ability.

MPD is a form of dissociation, but not the only one. Other categories of dissociation include psychogenic amnesia (temporary loss of memory), psychogenic fugue (sudden, unexpected travel away from one's home or customary place of work with an inability to recall the past), depersonalization disorder (feeling unreal, as in a dreamlike state), borderline personality disorder (unstable self-representation and interpersonal relationships), post-traumatic stress disorder (vivid traumatic memories) and dissociative disorders not otherwise specified (a wastebasket category for atypical MPD and all other forms of dissociation). Dissociation is also related to ego states, like the "inner child" that is often heard about in Adult Children of Alcoholics and similar groups. Ego states are found in normal and neurotic individuals as well as among those with dissociative disorders.

People are fascinated by multiple personality disorder. Books, criminal trials, tabloids and talk shows on MPD have captured the public imagination. Audiences have watched in horror and fascination the interviews with multiples; the viewers' attention is always focused on the most lurid and fearful details.

MPD taps into people's perception of what it must be like to be "possessed." Viewers want assurance that the multiple personalities are real and not faked; so alters are often "manifested" on the shows to prove their reality. The average viewer may be thinking, "Man alive! Think what I could get away with by saying that my alter did it." The multiple being interviewed and interrogated is thinking, "These people have no idea. They think I am putting this all on." Imagine her humiliation when she realizes that she has been exploited, laughed at and even booed by a titillated TV audience. Imagine how viewers with MPD feel: "They think she is a freak. If they knew me, they would think I am a freak, too. This is awful. Make them stop!" It feels like abuse all over again. Sometimes even their therapists participate shamelessly in this exploitation.

Audiences love sensationalism, and television gives them what they want to see: confused and frightened individuals suffering from an exotic malady. The public generally does not know that multiples are perfectly sane, creative and intelligent people for whom developing multiple personalities was the most effective way in childhood to cope with the inescapable horrors of their lives. Many MPDs hold down jobs and take care of their families without much appreciation for the incredible expenditure of emotional and psychic energy involved in doing so.

Talk show "guests" with MPD have been victims of horrendous and prolonged childhood abuse, generally from parents or close family members — certainly physical, and often sexual. For some individuals, cult-related abuse added a dimension of horror as it multiplied the traumatic effects exponentially in terms of occasions and perpetrators. In rare cases the trauma was unintended, as in cases of those who have suffered repeated surgery.

The average person with MPD has been in psychotherapy for six or seven years and has carried such diagnoses as depression, bipolar mood disorder, borderline personality disorder, schizophrenia, and even PMS. He or she has been medicated, analyzed, given electroconvulsive shock and hospitalized without anyone's having addressed the real dissociative problem.

Multiple personality disorder is finally being recognized again. We have learned more about this disorder in the past ten years than we have learned about any other mental health disorder in the past fifty. An abundance of research published in various professional journals clearly supports the designation of MPD as a valid diagnostic condition. Psychotherapists who refuse to recognize the diagnosis of MPD have not done their homework. It is no longer a matter of believing: it is a matter of keeping up to date on mental health research.

The 1987 *Diagnostic and Statistical Manual III-Revised* gives this "official" description of MPD:

> A. the existence within the person of two or more distinct personalities or personality states (each with its own relatively enduring pattern of perceiving, relating to, and thinking about the environment and self).
> B. At least two of these personalities or personality states recurrently take full control of the person's behavior.

In 1989, Ross described MPD as "A little girl imagining the abuse is happening to someone else." This is MPD in its simplest, most poignant form.

HOW MPD BEGINS

On the average the onset of multiple personalities occurs at about four years of age — which means that some children split much earlier and others split as late as their seventh year. However, without exception, MPD begins in childhood.

The personalities that "inhabit" the body of a multiple are most commonly called *alters*. An alter may be discrete and fully developed or may be a fragment, a partially developed personality. There is usually a host alter or executive self that interacts with the public, but none of the alters is the "real" or "true" personality. We will learn much more about this later.

Everyone knows that children have wonderful imaginations. They create playmates and wondrous scenarios. They go places and do things in their minds, naturally and innocently. Using that creative ability, a child who is tortured and terrified over a period of time may create other "children" who can take over, survive the torture and endure the pain. Other personalities may be formed to protect the child or help him cope with his horrors. These alter children may develop permanency, so that the identity of a single child fragments into that of many children in one body.

Once they were formed, survival, staying alive, fighting off torture and death was the sole purpose of these inner children (alters). They struggled to keep the self as intact as possible. Secrecy was crucial because — as their abusers warned them — talking would bring disaster. Secrecy, then, was a basic survival technique. To break the code of secrecy would bring pain or death or the murder of a loved one. Even without explicit threats, children realized that telling secrets might break up the family. Finally, telling meant having to acknowledge what had really happened. Abused children rarely tell. It is too dangerous and too shameful. The horrid memories get buried in the deep caves of the unconscious, each alter shielding his or her own traumatic memories from the others.

Creating multiple personalities was an excellent shield for the child. It was probably the only defense that would have worked. Quite often its effectiveness continued until the child became a young adult. Then the multiplicity ceased to work as an effective coping strategy, burdening the individual with amnesia, internal competition and confusion. Making decisions and following through on them became nearly impossible. The person was plagued with constant, unexplainable shame reactions, intrusive images, thought blockages, nightmares, medically undiagnosable pains and self-destructive behavior. Mood changes from depression to elation to rage to fear exhausted emotional resources and put impossible strains on interpersonal relationships. Just living from day to day required heroic effort. Thus, the effective coping strategy of childhood evolved into a nightmare of prolonged, ineffective medical and psychological treatment, and even repeated hospitalizations.

If multiple personality disorder is as common as those of us specializing in its treatment believe, many patients in mental health clinics are probably being inappropriately treated. Ross writes:

> I believe, based on preliminary research and clinical experience, that MPD is roughly as common as schizophrenia in North America. I think that two to five percent of psychiatric inpatients in North America in the late 1980s have full, classical MPD, in addition to a substantial number of outpatients who have the disorder. I think that MPD, psychogenic amnesia, and atypical dissociative disorder together are as common in the general population as the anxiety disorders.

In a later study, Ross found a 1.6 percent prevalence of MPD and an 11 percent prevalence of dissociative disorders among college students.

The good news for people with MPD is that it can be successfully treated. With the right attitude and effort on your part, combined with effective treatment, you can look forward to being one who *used to have* MPD. (You can then join those of us who have "singular personality disorder"!)

Inner Children
And Empty Chairs

"My friends in the adult survivors' group all have inner children that they can call out to play, and some of their inner children even have names. Do all these people have MPD? Does having an inner child make me a multiple?" These are pertinent questions. Many of us have watched John Bradshaw on television directing each member of the audience to close his or her eyes, breathe deeply, relax and contact the inner child. Some apparently found a child inside. Some of these inner children were happy and playful, but others were frightened, tearful and needed to be held and loved.

If you have ever observed a Gestalt therapy group, you have probably seen a participant talking to an inner self, for one Gestalt technique requires the client to visualize an inner self in an empty chair. The participant then talks, expresses feelings and negotiates with the self in the chair. Next the participant sits in the empty chair and role-plays the inner self, giving it a voice of its own. The "voice" in the empty chair comes alive with needs and feelings different from those of the more conscious self. With the discovery of this inner self, the participant has accessed an internal ego state akin to the inner child described by Bradshaw.

Many years ago I participated in a workshop with Fritz Perls, the founder of Gestalt therapy, and experienced first-hand this role-playing technique. Perls positioned me facing an empty chair. First, I played my "good" self, expressing dismay over the behavior of my "bad" self. Then I exchanged chairs and became the "bad" self and talked back to the "good" self. As I performed this exercise, my awareness of the group receded and I experienced the reality of both ego states. Through this dialogue my "good" and "bad" selves were able to negotiate some behaviors and resolve some of my internal conflicts.

We are all multiple in the sense that most of us have internal ego states that seem to have a life of their own. Philosophers have described the plurality of selves. Counselors talk about inner selves. Some psychologists and psychiatrists have described ego states. Those of us working with MPD are familiar with alter personalities. The professional literature on dissociation reflects a growing awareness of the inherent multiplicity within all of us. Ross summarized it well:

> The normal human mind is characterized by a greater degree of multiplicity than is generally thought to be the case in our culture. The problem with MPD is not the multiplicity as such. The problem in MPD is the abnormal personification of the "part-selves," the abnormal degree of amnesic barriers or failure of communication between the "part-selves," and the degree of conflict and dysfunction within the system.

As the field of dissociative studies matures, there will be even greater appreciation of philosophers and others who have long propounded the multiple nature of human beings.

The philosopher G. I. Gurdjieff is quoted as saying:

Man is a plural being. When we speak of ourselves ordinarily we speak of "I." We say " 'I' want to do this" — but this is a mistake.

There is no such "I," or rather there are hundreds, thousands of little "I's" in every one of us. We are divided in ourselves but we cannot recognize the plurality of our being except by observation and study. At one moment it is one "I" that acts, at the next moment it is another "I." It is because the "I's" in ourselves are contradictory that we do not function harmoniously.

P. D. Ouspensky, a colleague of Gurdjieff, elaborated on this point:

It is the greatest mistake to think that man is always one and the same. A man is never the same for long. He is continually changing. He seldom remains the same even for half an hour. We think that if a man is called Ivan he is always Ivan. Nothing of the kind. Now he is Ivan, in another minute he is Peter, and a minute later he is Nicholas, Sergius, Matthew, Simon. All of you think he is Ivan. You know that Ivan cannot do a certain thing. He cannot tell a lie, and you are surprised he could have done so. And, indeed, Ivan cannot lie; it is Nicholas who lied. And when the opportunity presents itself Nicholas *cannot help lying.* You will be astonished when you realize what a multitude of these Ivans and Nicholases live in one man. If you learn to observe them there is no need to go to a cinema.

The grandfather of ego state theory from the psychological perspective is John G. Watkins, who, in 1978, described a continuum of dissociation: On one end are people who have ego states like Bradshaw's inner children or Perl's inner selves. At the other end of the dissociation continuum are individuals with poly-fragmented multiple personality disorder.

The formation of ego states begins in infancy and probably continues throughout life. Creating ego states is a dissociative skill learned early and never forgotten; like other skills it may be used to avoid facing difficult situations. But individuals suffering with MPD may proliferate alter ego states long after the traumatic experiences of childhood and adolescence have passed, preventing the total personality from working through problems and so contributing further to the chaos and confusion of the MPD system.

Ego states may be of either gender and they perform various functions in support of the total personality. Although formed in childhood, the ego states may be of any age. Adult ego states formed in childhood, however, are always a child's version of what an adult should be; so the inner adults of childhood origin are usually very concrete and rigid caricatures. For instance, if there is an introjected mother who becomes a separate ego state, that mother remains forever the child's perception of mother. Even if the mother makes drastic changes in herself, the child's mother-ego state remains the same.

Ego states often arise from the internalization of parents — a "parental introject." Siblings may remark how much a brother reminds them of their father, or a sister may be exactly like their mother. Children absorb the rules, values, vocabulary and mannerisms of their parents. Parents, observed and absorbed into the psyche, become internal ego states that then assume a life of their own. Have you ever had the experience of doing something and hearing your mother's voice inside your head condemning or praising you? It was her voice, but you have made it your own.

Ego states become more rigid and mutually exclusive on the continuum from normal dissociation toward MPD. Psychologically healthy ego states blend together, share information and work together for the good of the whole personality. Toward the dysfunctional end of the continuum, there is less blending in reaction to specific situations and more struggle between the ego states for dominance.

At some point along the continuum of increased dissociation, the individual stops thinking of the ego states as parts of self and begins to think of them as other. The inner child ceases to be the collection of feelings and perceptions that most people have and becomes Billy or Janie or little Josephine. At the point where ego states are no longer acknowledged as part of the whole self, they tend to create problems for the adult. Operating independently, with their own agendas, the dissociated ego states can create the kind of chaos typical among MPDs.

MPD ego states are rigidly divided into discrete alter personalities sharing one body. When one ego state/alter personality assumes executive control of the body, the others are usually excluded from consciousness. You may then know the despair, confusion and embarrassment of discovering that various parts of you have been acting independently, secretly and at cross purposes. Such is the experience of an individual with MPD.

The more open and permeable ego states give color, depth, variety and spontaneity to the total personality. They are formed as the child interacts with life situations, discovering that certain patterns of behavior are more effective than others in need gratification or defense or for solving specific problems. Sometimes it is best to be helpless and innocent like a toddler. At other times one must be a "little man" or a "little mother." Once learned, these patterns tend to persist and to influence us the rest of our lives. How many adults have you known who have a petulant child inside? They may have tantrums that remind you of four-year-olds stamping their feet and raging.

When a child lives in a dysfunctional home, there is more likelihood of the development of discrete inner children who provide survival skills. To ensure the physical and psychological survival of the total personality, it becomes necessary for the personality to differentiate such functions as defensive skills and survival behaviors at higher and higher levels. Sometimes important coping behaviors are mutually inconsistent. A child may need to be a willing sex partner for father, a perfect little lady for mother, a truthful Christian girl for the church and a facile liar to protect family secrets — all at the same time. The ego states provide an excellent mechanism for doing so. When the family dysfunction includes abuse, the separation of ego states increases.

If the abuse approaches the level of torture and terror at which survival is questionable, the child may develop the discrete and rigidly separated alter personalities found in MPD. Effective survival strategies for the child require that alters be able to perform with independence and in secret from each other.

Inner children and the empty chairs of Gestalt therapy can complicate the diagnosis of MPD. Your therapist will help you uncover your ego states and will examine with you the rigidity and impermeability of their boundaries. Remember that childhood trauma and lost memories (amnesia) are key for a diagnosis of MPD.

In the next chapter we will examine the ways in which individuals with MPD describe themselves. The symptoms mentioned will be common to many and are not unique to any one person.

FOUR

Am I MPD?

Clammy hands and panicky feelings are typical when you confront the question, "Am I MPD?" This book cannot make a diagnosis, but here are the symptoms of multiplicity. You can be your own judge.

Certain feelings and experiences are common to people with multiple personalities. Most MPD individuals are aware of pervasive and faceless fear, unreasonable fear, fear that often evolves into terror. They also have large blocks of missing memories. Amnesia is the hallmark of secrecy, the main tool for survival during the times of terror and abuse.

Until you begin to understand your own multiple system, you will probably be unaware of the big role that secrecy has played in your life. You may be vaguely aware of having no memory of large blocks of your childhood and adolescence, but you probably have not thought much about it. Maybe you have assumed that everyone has sparse early memories. Only after delving into your past will you realize that you indeed have childhood memories, that they are blocked and inaccessible. Early traumatic events may be dissociated until adulthood, when fragments of memory begin to surface.

The constant fearfulness and scarcity of childhood recollections are common to multiples. Usually grief, depression, distrust, shame and rage accompany the fear. Since these strong emotions are not consciously connected to childhood trauma, they are frequently experienced as alien; the feelings do not seem to be related to anything real. Multiples often wonder whether they are crazy or have a brain tumor.

The purpose of this chapter is to clarify the role of these feelings and motivations in your life if you have MPD. You may recognize yourself in these descriptions, but the life-long pattern of internal and external secrecy may complicate your acceptance of the MPD diagnosis.

Most clients, well along in treatment, periodically doubt that they are multiples. Your second thoughts about the diagnosis are to be expected. You may not want anyone to know your diagnosis. You probably have vivid memories of the way multiples have been treated by the public. You may prefer not to know the hard truth of your MPD. Early in therapy you probably did not want even your therapist to know about your multiple personalities. Very few clients enter psychotherapy admitting that they have the disorder. Friends may recognize the multiplicity and urge treatment, but the client, not wanting to be labeled "crazy," may deliberately try to mislead the therapist into a more "standard" psychological diagnosis. Denial is alive and well in the world of dissociation.

Be forewarned that no one symptom makes you a multiple. Typical emotional, behavioral, neurophysiological and cognitive MPD symptoms, seen separately, are also characteristic of other diagnoses. All your experiences are important, but only one is crucial for a diagnosis of multiple personality disorder — the existence of mutually amnesic alter personalities that, from time to time, take executive control of the body. Your therapist cannot make a definitive diagnosis of MPD unless he or she meets at least one of your alters directly.

No two clients with MPD are alike. The most common form of MPD is atypical MPD. It worries some clients that they are not like the well-publicized Sybil, Eve or Billy. Think about it. When the traumatized child developed alter personalities, she did not have a handbook to go by. She did it her own way, the way it made sense to her, the way she needed to do it for her own survival. If you are multiple, you are exactly right in doing it your way.

A few readers will have all the experiences described below, while others will have only a few. Each person's experience will be unique. There is no right or wrong way to relive a past traumatic event. Accept your memories and behaviors as contributions of the alter personalities to the *whole* of you. Each personality was doing its very best to keep your system intact. Some shielded memories. Others carried positive or negative emotions. Some alters were guardians and protectors. The behavior of each was a gift to all. It is difficult to value the contributions of the alters when they seem to cause you so much pain, but the inner workings of your personality system assured your survival. Your ultimate survival was their gift to you.

PREVIOUS THERAPY

Most multiples will have been through six or seven years of therapy, often with several therapists. The previous psychologist or psychiatrist will have made a diagnosis based on presenting symptoms and probably felt confident about it.

Imagine that all of your previous therapists have come together to consult on your diagnosis. They sit around a table, your records stacked in front of each one. The chairperson greets everyone, makes sure all are comfortable and calls the meeting to order. "My thanks to each one of you for taking time from your busy schedules to be here today. Our task is to put our heads together and settle on a definitive diagnosis for Mrs. X. She is a very complex case, and from what I can gather each one of us has seen her in a different way. Dr. Z, may we start with you?"

"Yes, glad to begin. I saw Mrs. X for a period of six months. She was extremely depressed and suffered greatly. There were whole days when she would stay in bed. She was weepy. She had no energy. She lost interest in everything. I placed her on a regimen of antidepressants, and she saw my social worker for counseling each week. Mrs. X showed only modest improvement, and she dropped out of therapy."

Dr. B adds, "Yes, I saw her depression, but it was not so bad when she came to me. I was more impressed by the quality of her anxiety. She was experiencing panic states and was terrified of losing control. She was going from crisis to crisis, and we could find no reason for her agitation. I think she is suffering more from a generalized anxiety disorder. I put her on a course of medications, but they didn't seem to help much. I don't know what happened to her. She just stopped keeping her appointments."

Psychologist Dr. G sits forward: "But did you ever see her become manic? She came to me complaining of depression, worried about everything. She didn't mention panic attacks, but within a week she was feeling great, on top of the world — no depression, no problems, no need for meds. She was a very impulsive lady with grandiose ideas . . . totally unrealistic. I think we have a manic-depressive disorder here."

Sitting across the table, therapist M smiles knowingly. She speaks with authority: "What we have here is a borderline personality disorder who has managed to fool all of you. She has the classic features. She runs "hot" or "cold" in her relationships. Her love turns to hate faster than an eye blink. I have seen her love and hate her husband in the same sentence almost. She isn't anchored anywhere. She couldn't decide whether I was the worst counselor in the world or the mother she always wanted. Her therapy must give her structure and help her learn to adapt to the real world. Unfortunately she got angry at me and did not return; so I wasn't able to help her."

Psychologist D, sitting next to her, chimes in, "That may be, although I am not sure I agree with you. I was impressed by her obsessive-compulsive features. She had all the ritual behavior and repetitious thoughts that one would expect. She complained she felt as if the same tape was running over and over in her head. I had her set up for therapy and meds, but she did not come back. I think she is obsessive-compulsive, but I was not able to develop a therapeutic alliance with her."

Psychiatrist A, who once saw her in the hospital, says, "This lady is obviously schizophrenic. She hears voices. They tell her what to do. They constantly put her down. The voices even debate each other. More than that, she sat in the office one day and argued with me that she was a slender blond with blue eyes; as you all know, she is a stocky brunette. The lady is patently psychotic. Schizophrenia. That's it."

The consult continues. Each therapist describes what he or she has seen in the client, and each is partially correct. The chairperson insists that they agree upon a diagnosis, and finally, after lengthy and sometimes heated discussion, they do: "Mrs. X is a schizophrenic with manic-depressive features and borderline characteristics and seems to have developed obsessive-compulsive strategies to bind her anxiety." Having finished their work, they shake hands, gather up their files and return to their busy practices.

Of course, the above diagnosis is nonsense. Surely no group of mental health professionals would ever come up with such a thing. If you were to compile all the diagnoses given you in the past, however, it might look very much like the pseudodiagnosis prepared by our imaginary panel.

As a multiple, you may have most of these symptoms or all of them. You can see how you might have been given many different diagnoses and medications. If your therapist is not up to date with the professional literature on dissociation, he or she most likely missed the diagnosis of MPD by not looking for it.

QUESTIONS TO ASK YOURSELF

The truth is that even the most experienced and knowledgeable therapist will sometimes miss MPD, for it can hide behind the mask of several other disorders and it can be hidden by a client determined to keep secrets. The symptoms mentioned above are common to MPDs, but without manifested alters these symptoms alone cannot identify you as having multiple personality disorder.

Here are some questions to ask yourself:

- **Do you have any memories of your childhood?** If you have few or no memories before the age of 15, for example, you might wonder why.
- **Do you have any memory of being abused as a child?** Sometimes you will have a fragmentary memory of abuse, a strong feeling, intrusive images, body sensations that are triggered. Sometimes you will actually have knowledge of what happened, but many times you will have no memory at all of the traumatic events.
- **Do you lose time?** Many multiples cannot account for blocks of time — such as what happened this morning, yesterday afternoon, last Saturday. You may have the disconcerting experience of having an acquaintance talk about a shared experience of which you have no recollection. Or you may find strangers thanking you for (or accusing you of) things totally unknown to you. You may even discover that you have enrolled in a course or taken a job and have no memory of having done so. Perhaps you have "awakened" in a neighboring town without a notion of why or how you made the trip. Such *repeated* amnesic experiences are suggestive of MPD.

  A second, less frequently mentioned form of amnesia has been described by Adam Crabtree — and *identity amnesia* is perhaps more common than the *event amnesia* mentioned above. With identity amnesia you are aware of the event — of the trip, of your behavior; you remember its happening and you observed it, but it did not feel as if *you* were there. Someone else was the actor, and you were an observer. You were co-conscious but not involved. This form of amnesia, very common in MPD, is also found in less seriously dissociated individuals.

- **Do you find yourself engaging in uncharacteristic behaviors (identity amnesia), or do others tell you that you sometimes act in ways uncharacteristic of you and you cannot imagine what they are talking about (event amnesia)?** It is common for spouses and children of multiples never to know "who" is going to meet them at home after work or school. They might be coldly ignored, cursed, punished or bedded and have no idea what set off the behaviors.
- **Do you experience irresistible urges to cut or burn yourself?** Do these urges follow in the wake of strong emotions, such as anger or sadness? Sometimes, even after a happy occasion, an MPD client will experience an episode of self-mutilation, as if something or someone inside cannot stand for the self to be happy. Or some kind of everyday stress will be followed by a compulsion to self-mutilate or commit suicide, as if self-destruction is the only possible response to stress.
- **Do you have secret names that you go by at different times?** Maybe at work you like to be called by one name, a different name in your group, and still another name at home. Are you aware of different people inside yourself who have their own names? Secret names are very suggestive of MPD.
- **Do you experience flashbacks or spontaneous abreactions?** Some professionals believe that flashbacks and abreactions are the same thing. Others believe that they are a little different. For my purposes I call a *flashback* a vivid memory of either part or all of a traumatic experience and an *abreaction* a reliving of the total experience.

  Most multiples have flashbacks and abreactions that are highly disturbing to them. They see enough to upset them, but not enough to recover the entire experience. They may remember a place and know that something terrible happened there, but not know what.
- **Do you commonly have vivid nightmares?** Such dreams are often memories in the form of a metaphor. They will raise many associated emotions, and sometimes dreams are true abreactions of trauma.
- **Do you experience sudden and unexpected physical sensations?** These might include a sharp pain in the genitals, a tightness in the throat or a clamping feeling around the arms. Perhaps these are *body memories* (partial abreactions in which only the physical sensations are revived). Such

sensations can be very disconcerting if they happen while you are working or involved in a social situation. Body memories can even leave stigmata — for example, cigarette burns from childhood may unaccountably reappear on your body. In such cases an alter may be trying to abreact or share a memory without exposing the emotional or cognitive content.

Flashbacks and abreactions are common to dissociative disorders, but by themselves they do not warrant the diagnosis of multiple personality disorder.

- **Do you suffer from severe headaches that are as painful as migraines and may even have been medically diagnosed as migraines?** Everyone has headaches, but the headaches of an MPD individual often begin and end abruptly. While the pain lasts, the head feels as if it will explode. In MPD such headaches are usually caused by a struggle between one or more alters for control.
- **Have you been treated for seizures?** Pseudoseizures are common among individuals with MPD. You may have been taking Dilantin or other seizure medication for years, only to find that the seizures disappear as treatment progresses. Pseudoseizures appear to be related to power struggles among the alters. If you have seizures, your therapist should recommend a thorough neurological evaluation with an overnight EEG.
- **Has your personal physician noticed physical evidence of childhood trauma, such as vaginal or other kinds of scarring?** If you have had unbelievable memory fragments of childhood sexual trauma, your gynecologist's observations may help you trust your memories and encourage you to get on with your therapy.

ALTER PERSONALITIES

The one sign necessary for a diagnosis of MPD is the existence of discrete alter personalities that have a life of their own and sometimes take control of the body. You may not know them directly, but you may be aware of many internal arguments and running commentary that add to your cognitive confusion. You may also experience amnesic blank spots in your daily life.

Alters come in all ages and both genders, so there may be child, adolescent and adult alters of either sex. Certain alters may be cooperative and open to therapy, while others may be suspicious, wary and hostile. In any case, each alter is as much the client as is the host personality. All must find their place in the therapy process.

SYMPTOMS

Richard Kluft, arguably the world's foremost MPD therapist, compiled the following list of signs suggesting MPD:

- prior treatment failure
- three or more prior diagnoses
- concurrent psychiatric and somatic symptoms
- fluctuating symptoms and level of function
- severe headaches
- time distortion or time lapses
- being told of disremembered behaviors
- others noting observable changes
- discovery of productions, objects or handwriting in one's possession that one cannot account for or recognize.
- the hearing of voices (more than 80 percent experienced as within the head), experienced as separate, urging toward some good or bad activity
- the use of "we" in a collective sense
- the elicitability of other alters through hypnosis and/or Amytal.

As you look back over this chapter, you may recognize yourself. If what you have read seems to fit you, then find a therapist trained to work with dissociative disorders and get a professional opinion. The good news is that MPD can be successfully treated. It will take time and great effort, but you will be able to look forward to a life without therapy, without psychotropic medication and without the unremitting misery, confusion, shame and embarrassment caused by trauma and concealed within multiplicity.

FIVE

The Princess Of The Dark Cloak

A Story by Priscilla Cogan

Once upon a time there lived a little girl
With dark hair and a sweet smile
And a wish that everybody would like her.
This little girl was a princess who lived
In a dark, dank castle — not at all like the beautiful
Castles in the fairy tale books.
She lived in the dark, sooty castle with her family —
The King, the Queen, brothers and sisters, and just
Lots of people and lots of noise.
There were few places this little girl could find
Peace and Quiet except in her books, her daydreams
And her lively imagination.
On rare occasions the sun would peek out
Through the clouds,
Over the castle walls, and bathe her in the golden light.
And oh! this little girl would tuck that in her memory
To make it last all that much longer, the warming sun.

For love was to her like the warming sun, to hold,
To treasure, to keep alive
Even in the midst of the darkest day
And the dampest night.
Her mind worked overhard in thinking of ways
To keep the sun shining,
To make others love her and hardest of all,
In the midst of the darkness, to find ways
She could keep that sun close to her heart, so that she could love.

But the nights were cruel and winter was overlong.
The little girl found herself growing colder and colder,
As the dampness soaked into her very being,
As the wind whipped mercilessly about her bare legs.
The King and Queen were so busy with their own world
They didn't even notice that their little girl's clothes
Were tattered and torn,
And she was afraid to tell them, lest they get angry with her.

For this little princess was Very Afraid of their anger,
For like all royalty, the King and Queen
Were very demanding
And not the least bit sympathetic to their subjects
Nor their children.
For like many rulers, they were very imperial
In their demands,
Commanding their people to do this, do that,
Act in this way,
Act in that way.
Why they even demanded that Everyone feel, think and do Just
As they commanded.
The little girl soon discovered that if she had a feeling,
Or a thought all her own,
The King would say, "Humbug, that's not right! What do you
know?"
And then proceeded to tell her what Was right.
The Queen would say, "You're just a little girl.
Of course, you don't feel that way. Who ever heard of such a
thing? Why it's just your imagination!"

This left the little girl very, very confused
And very, very afraid because the world
Was not what it seemed to be
According to her feelings,
Her thoughts, her perceptions.

So she quickly learned that it wasn't safe to tell people
What she saw, what she felt, what she knew to be true
And keeping it all inside, the little girl discovered
An even more bitter cold
As she faced the outside world.

Despite the freeze and the bitter cold,
She didn't die,
She fought to survive.

She found a cloak of just the right size
For her small, shivering body
A cloak that was all black on the outside
In which she could hide;
A place of safety and warmth,
And all red on the inside,
A warm color, the color of the hot sun
With which she surrounded herself.
Wrapped in this cloak, the little girl knew
She was safe.

The black cloak disguised her feelings well,
So that the King and Queen didn't punish her as much
Or even notice her that much;
The little girl kept secret the brilliant red,
Wrapping it tightly about her
To keep her warm in the fires of the heart.

It was also a cloak of many pockets,
Big pockets and small pockets
All contained within the inner red lining
That nobody but our little princess knew about.
And like all little girls, she would collect things

And stash them in her pockets, until even she
Forgot about them.

When something made her sad, a harsh word,
A look of contempt, she'd take the blue mood
And stuff it into one of her pockets,
So as to keep it hidden from everyone Out There.
Or when she'd feel purplish with rage,
Wanting to strike out and hurt those
Who hurt her, she'd take that, too,
And stuff it into an inner pocket.

Her pockets grew full with all their stuffings.
When lonely, the little girl would create a playmate,
That only she knew she had,
To play with, to talk to, to laugh with, in secret
And when with others, knowing better,
The little girl stuck her playmate in a pocket
For future use.
She was quite clever because all on her own
She held true to her feelings, her perceptions,
Only keeping them hidden from Out There.

Time passed, and the princess began slowly to blossom
As all little girls do.
In Spring she felt the first stirrings of life,
Of creation, of sensuality
As the flowers opened up their buds
From the long winter nap.

Yet no one —
Not the Queen, not the King,
No one — told her about all these new feelings stirring up
Inside her,
And so that, too, she learned to guard
And pocket deep inside of herself.
No one knew of the spring inside her,
The wild rush of life.
All they knew was the Princess of the Dark Cloak.

Pretty soon there were young men coming round the castle door,
Wanting to meet the Princess of the Dark Cloak.
There were things she had to learn.
And she became busy and busier the older she grew.
So busy that all the stuffed pockets of
This and that,
Old feelings, old playmates,
Old parts of herself
Were soon forgotten.

And like all princesses, eventually this one wed
Her prince
And left the big, dark, noisy, gloomy castle
To find a home of greater sunshine
And more love than she thought possible.

Known as the Princess of the Dark Cloak,
She kept it as her trademark,
So that everyone would know who she was,
Even though it was awfully small for an adult
And awfully lumpy with all those stuffed inner pockets
And slowly fraying on the edge from so many years of wear and
    tear.

Until there came a day, a long time after leaving home,
She walked by a mirror and perchance saw herself
In the old cloak.
For lately she had been finding it hard to move about,
Increasingly difficult to breathe,
As if she were smothering or choking,
All tight inside and constricted.
She looked in the mirror to make sure
That ropes didn't bind her arms,
As everything began to press in on her
And scare her.

In the mirror she saw how small was her cloak
And how big she had grown,

How the buttons in front could barely keep from popping,
How her arms extended way beyond the sleeves and
Her knees appeared exposed.
Most of all she saw how tight the cloak bound her
So that she couldn't breathe right.
It was heavy, so heavy that it exhausted her
To wear it, but she had quite forgotten the pockets
Crammed with this and crammed with that.

Now being the Princess of the Dark Cloak,
She had never, never taken it off.
For hadn't the cloak been the very thing to save her life
In the time of the Bitter Cold?
So, as she looked at her reflection,
She didn't know what to do.

At first she just wished the pain,
The tightness of breath
Would disappear,
That somehow the cloak would magically enlarge
And give her room to move about in.
But wishing is wishing,
And wishing didn't
Remove the heaviness that had settled into her.
Then she decided just to live with the pain,
And for a very, very long time she struggled with
The cloak's weight and increasing heaviness
Until all her joints hurt,
And still the cloak bound her too tightly.
For it was a child's cloak, and
the princess had become a woman.

Doctors from far and wide
Came and gave her drugs,
To kill the pain,
To give her sleep,
But none looked beyond the Princess of the Dark Cloak
To the real problem, underneath.

Finally an old woman appeared,
For she saw the princess was in pain
And was scared and confused and feeling all alone.
The princess besought this old woman to help her,
For the pain was growing worse
And the heaviness unbearable.

The old woman of many wrinkles
Told her that deep inside the cloak were many pockets,
All stuffed with bits and pieces from the princess' life.
Blue fabric from the times of deep sadness, purple
From the times of rage, old playmates from the time of
Childhood, protectors from the time of dark pain.
Pockets and pockets, frozen in time,
Forgotten by her a long time ago.
The old woman told her the heaviness came from carrying
All this unattached weight,
Instead of wearing it.

The princess studied this old woman carefully,
Wondering indeed if this woman was just a doddering old fool
Or if she really knew something about her
That she had forgotten.
Warily, cautiously, the princess inquired,
"How do I get rid of this tiredness, this unattached weight?"
Then she studied the old woman, in uncertain disbelief.

It took a long time for the old woman to answer,
A thoughtful time.
She warned the Princess,
"It will take a long time, to grow free of this forgetting.
It will take a long time to forget to fear.
It will take a long time to remember
That before the Princess of the Dark Cloak
There was the princess,
And that the cloak was just a mantle to cover her
And keep out the bitter cold."

The old woman chided her,
"You look in the mirror, my princess
And see for yourself the Princess of the Dark Cloak.
I look in the same mirror
And see the princess, you."

The princess now was very confused;
Not knowing the difference in the mirror's reflection.

Still the old woman spoke,
"It will take a long time
And you will need to learn to sew, and stitch, and seam,
For inside of those forgotten pockets are all
The bits and pieces of you,
Frozen in time, forgotten in time,
Just jammed down deep and covered up
By your black cloak.
Slowly, you must examine these pockets,
Pull out their contents, remember them,
Give them your respect, for they are parts of you,
Needing to be honored,
Needing to be updated.
Those parts which are useful to This time, This place,
You must take and sew into the fabric of your cloak,
Into the fabric of your being,
So that the cloak becomes a rainbow of colors."

Still these words frightened, nay, terrified the princess
Because, at least, she KNEW the dark cloak well.
Her parents, her husband, her friends all knew her well
As the Princess of the Dark Cloak.
The dark cloak had fitted well in the darkness
Of her childhood castle,
But she was not one to wear her feelings on her sleeve.

The old woman sensed her terror and spoke of it,
"Yes, my dear, it is frightening to think that one can't
Stitch the fabric, unless the cloak is off
And before you.

You still fear the cold, the bitter winds,
You doubt today's sunshine and tomorrow's dawn.
At times you seek the darkness of sleep
Before the darkness of anticipation.
There is pain in remembering, but remember this too:
The pockets contain sunshine as well as sadness,
Joy and playfulness as well as rage,
Moments of triumph as well as pain,
Old friends as well as enemies."

The princess listened thoughtfully to these words,
So full of questions and confusion,
Wanting to forget,
Wanting to remember,
And mostly just feeling dread of old dank castles
And dark times.
"How do I begin? Where do I find a thread strong enough?
What will the cloak look like when I'm finished with it?
And where will I find the courage to do this?"

The old woman smiled and replied,
"The little girl is our beginning,
The little girl before the dark cloak with all the pockets,
Before all the forgettings,
The little girl who lives in the dark castle.
We will pick her up and hold her close.
We will protect her and bring her
Into the sunshine of today;
You and I will love this little girl,
This little girl who is you.
She is our beginning,
But the thread we use is not that of a child's stitching.
The thread we will use will be that of an adult
Who has grown strong over the years
And stands on her own two feet,
Under no one's dominion but her own.
The courage is there, too, deep inside the pockets.
It is the courage of one who has survived.
We must honor that courage, you and I."

The old woman continued,
"The new cloak will be a long time in the making,
Full of new and startling colors,
No longer just a solid steady black.
It will be a cloak big enough to wrap all the way Around you
And still give you room to grow in,
To breathe freely,
To love in and be loved.
It will be a cloak without gaps and hidden pockets,
But one that honors you and what you have experienced.
It will be not just a cloak of history,
But a cloak of today and for your future."

The princess knew down deep
That when she was very, very young
She had found a way to capture a piece of sunlight
And put it close to her heart,
To warm her and keep her safe in the darkness.
Now the darkness felt as if it were gaining on her
Except for the words of the old woman
Who promised her the sun,
With all its glare,
But all its warmth,
If she set forth on the task before her.

You little ones who have just heard this story may feel
that you, too, live in a tight coat with lots of pockets and
hidden places. It may feel warm and less frightening inside
the coat where it is dark, but it is also tight and hard to
breathe in there.

Sunshine is wonderful. Feeling safe may take a while,
but you will learn that your days of pain and abuse are
over. Like the Princess of the Dark Cloak, your body has
grown too big for your old coat and you, like the princess,
will come out to live in the light.

Therapists And Therapy For MPD?

If you suspect that you have multiple personality disorder and you are in therapy under another diagnosis, you *must* share your suspicions with your therapist. If your therapist is willing to examine this possibility with you, then therapy can proceed. However, there are many mental health professionals who have not kept up with the field and are unaware of the research that clearly defines MPD and outlines effective treatment approaches. The therapeutic strategies mentioned in this chapter are based primarily upon the work of Richard Kluft, whose exhaustive clinical research and teaching are indispensable in this field.

If your therapist does not recognize MPD as a valid diagnosis and is unwilling to learn, you will need to find another therapist. Otherwise your psychotherapeutic journey will be endless, and you will never get well. That is the hard truth. If you are diabetic, treating circulation problems will not help unless the diabetes is addressed; and if your doctor does not "believe" in diabetes, you had better get a doctor who does. This analogy is imperfect because MPD is not a disease, but the principle is the same. There is no record of MPD having ever been cured by treating symptoms only or by forcing the repression of alter personalities.

Your first step should be to look for a psychotherapist who is familiar with dissociative disorders and who has taken special training in treating MPD, is getting that training or is willing to further his or her education in the area. Unfortunately, few mental health professionals will have received such training in their degree programs.

Whether your therapist is a psychologist, a psychiatrist, a psychiatric nurse, a mental health counselor or a psychiatric social worker is less important than whether he or she has been trained in the diagnosis and treatment of MPD. *You have the right and obligation to yourself to inquire about the basic training and skills of your prospective therapist.* Ask! If that therapist doesn't have them, call someone else. You may also call the International Society for the Study of Multiple Personality and Dissociation (ISSMP&D) in Skokie, Illinois, to ask if there is a professional member in your vicinity. The ISSMP&D cannot guarantee that a particular member is competent to treat MPD, but a professional member should at least be familiar with the disorder and should be able to make a referral.

You will need a therapist who will be available for several years; so do not begin work with an intern or a therapist who will be moving away before your therapy is complete. Unfortunately, psychotherapists in public mental health clinics tend to have a short tenure. Again, ask. Your finances may dictate that you seek help through a public agency. If this is the case, attempt to find a psychotherapist who will be available for several more years. Abandonment is usually a big issue with multiples, and having to change therapists midstream can be a real hardship.

Your early sessions in therapy will give you time to develop a working relationship with your therapist. It is important that you feel comfortable enough to talk frankly with this person and allow trust to grow. Trust and control are going to be big issues for you. Parts of you will not be trustful for a long time. After all, you were probably abused by individuals who were supposed to take care of you. However, you will soon be able to tell if yours is a counselor with whom trust can grow. Be a good mental health consumer. If your therapist is not the one who can help you; look elsewhere. It is vital that the "fit" be just right.

During the early sessions, you and your therapist will be working toward an accurate diagnosis. Alternative diagnoses must be ruled out. If you have multiple personality disorder, the next step will be for you to accept the diagnosis, roll up your sleeves and prepare to work.

HYPNOSIS

Hypnosis is a basic and universal tool in treating MPD. Those with experience in the field are in consensus that effective treatment requires it — and there are logical reasons for this. Anyone with a dissociative disorder is, by definition, a virtuoso in hypnosis. Hypnosis is a voluntary form of dissociation. As a multiple you are in trance states every day, and through hypnosis your inner personality system may be more easily accessed. Indeed, multiples typically use self-hypnotic switching techniques, often without being aware of doing so. Hypnosis will become crucially important during the abreactive phase of treatment because it will let you recall and integrate memories without being overwhelmed by affect or retraumatized by the process. There is no adequate substitute for hypnosis.

While hypnosis will be the most valuable tool used in your therapy, it may initially raise control and trust issues for you. Your therapist will have to address these issues directly and honestly. Dispelling myths about hypnotic control and educating yourself will help you to understand that it is a natural process. Ask for a book about self- or therapeutic hypnosis. If hypnosis continues to be a control issue for you, therapy will be significantly impeded.

As a treatment tool, hypnosis will save both you and the therapist valuable time and will be your greatest protection as it slows down the release of memories, stops uncontrolled abreactions and teaches you ways of restoring order within your personality system.

The first goal of therapy is to establish a therapeutic alliance — which can take a long time, even years, depending on the complexity and cooperation of your personality system. Once an adequate alliance is established, your therapist will want you to map the system of personalities. He or she will need to know the individual alters, the purpose each serves and, in general terms, what each has experienced. The child alters are the ones who most often carry memories of abuse, while the adult alters often serve as protectors and protagonists. The alters play different roles. If you could see an overview of the whole system, you would understand how each personality has been necessary for the protection and preservation of the whole.

Not all alters are friendly to outsiders or even to each other. Typically some will be persecutors who had initially attempted to protect the system but were overwhelmed by trauma. Their next strategy for survival was to identify with the abusers, to help the system anticipate future abuse. Such alters maintain the old pattern of abuse because they don't recognize that the living situation has changed. Nevertheless, every one of your parts is important and essential to you. Each has played a role in protecting you and in making you a survivor. Be assured that none of them will be ignored, sloughed off or destroyed. When therapy ends, each one will be represented in the whole.

Every alter needs to know that change is possible. Often alters are relatively narrow in scope, trapped in old times and old strategies: they hold particular memories, carry certain feelings or perform some very specific function. They will grow, change, develop new talents and facets and become fuller beings. The inevitability of change is demonstrated, for example, when a rageful alter begins to discover that he or she can be more thoughtful and avoid angry responses or experience other emotions, such as playfulness and sadness. As the alters move toward health, the amnesic barriers between them lose their importance and become permeable. Thus, MPD alter personalities evolve into healthy ego states.

Many therapists write down the names of the alters and group them by "families," traits or interests — a necessity for the therapist who has many MPD clients. You can imagine how many names have to be remembered, and how many names will be duplicated among the clients.

As you read about MPD, you may be surprised by the number of personalities attributed to different individuals. There may be as few as two or three, and there may be thousands; the average number is about thirteen.

You might expect a person with a great number of alters to have a bleak prognosis for treatment. That is not necessarily so. Success in treatment has less to do with the number of alters than with your commitment to stay in therapy until you are integrated and prepared to live effectively in your new wholeness.

An optimal therapy schedule is two or three sessions a week; some therapists will schedule one double session and one single session each week. Obviously your insurance, your insurer's treatment review system and your personal financial resources will play a part in determining your program.

After you and your therapist have established the diagnosis, mapped the system and taken an intellectual review of your history, treatment will focus on techniques of mastery within the family of alters. Early therapeutic work must be dedicated to moving the MPD alters down the dissociation continuum (see Chapter 2) toward a more open, less defended ego state system. *This is the most important part of early therapy because it is a necessary prerequisite for later memory retrieval.*

In the early days of modern MPD therapy, treatment usually consisted of opening up the system and abreacting the traumatic memories as soon as a therapeutic alliance was developed. The abreactions, however, tended to be incomplete. The client would become overwhelmed by memory; the alters would become immobilized or withdrawn and the whole system would be left in an unresolved state of trauma: that is, the client would be retraumatized.

Your therapist will help you process any significant memories that have already surfaced. Then he or she will work with the system to develop constructive techniques to cope with horrendous memories without your becoming overwhelmed and dysfunctional. There are strategies for opening and closing abreactions.

You can learn to withdraw to a "safe place" that is unique to each personality when you feel you are at the mercy of surfacing memories, or you may bank-vault overwhelming emotions and keep them locked away for processing at a later date. You may contain your experiences in a "visualized" book of personal history that you can open and close as you are prepared to process your memories. It will not be easy or pleasant to reclaim your horrific memories, but your therapist can help you control the process so that you are not retraumatized. Hypnosis is indispensable in helping you develop and refine these safety procedures. Some specialists in the field claim that hypnosis is best used not to aid in the recovery of memory, but to slow down the emergence of memories so that one is not overwhelmed and retraumatized.

GROUP THERAPY

Your therapist will probably advise you against adjunctive group therapy unless such therapy is an integral part of the treatment plan. This recommendation against group therapy is particularly warranted if emotional catharsis is the style of the group. MPD therapy must be focused first on mastery and finally on full and complete abreactions brought about in a way that protects the system from retraumatization.

Many MPD clients report that nonintrusive support groups — Alcoholics Anonymous, Adult Children of Alcoholics, Survivors of Incest Anonymous and 12-Step MPD groups — are a real source of comfort to them; however, there seems to be a growing consensus among therapists treating MPD that participation in these groups may actually complicate and slow down therapy. These groups are wonderful for many survivors, but perhaps are not so helpful for survivors with MPD. Twelve-Step groups emphasize doing memory work by yourself and then sharing your memories with the group, and so there is an implicit demand to produce memories to share; if you aren't coming up with memories, you are not doing the work. Forcing memory work before the MPD system is prepared for it may allow resistant alters to have a field day leading you around in circles, disguising themselves as "higher powers," and generally frustrating your best efforts. Real competition often develops as a group participant strives to demonstrate that he or she is the most complex multiple, is the most committed to recovering traumatic memories, or is the most knowledgeable about dealing with MPD. Participants also run the risk of becoming enmeshed in one anothers' lives. Loose boundaries are a common problem among multiples. When a whole group of multiples begins to incorporate each other within personal and psychological boundaries, therapeutic contamination is bound to result.

You will probably agree that your problems are enough, that having an alter take on an additional problem as his own will be too much. Think about a child alter trying to make sense of his trauma, unable to understand the experience or even how it happened. What happens to this child alter when he hears an MPD or Survivors' group member recount some gruesome memory? Inner children do not have intact boundaries. Typically they cannot separate the emotions and memories of other people from their own. So when a child part of you hears about trauma from someone else, it can become confused and take on trauma that does not belong to you. You may actually "borrow" someone else's experiences as a metaphor to clothe your own. It is no coincidence that when one member of an MPD group recounts a certain kind of experience, other members are "remembering," within a week, that they too had that experience. This does not invalidate anyone's traumatic experiences, but it suggests that someone else's story may shape the way you perceive your own trauma. So, if you want support, choose your group wisely and remember that your expression of multiplicity is uniquely yours and different from that of everyone else. Always be aware that your boundaries may be violated in many subtle ways.

You may have discovered your multiplicity through a support group. This book does not necessarily advocate your turning away from groups and friends that have been close to you. Just be aware that your therapy will go better for you and be less traumatic if you follow the proven MPD therapy, if you leave the ACoA/SIA approaches to nonmultiples and work diligently at maintaining your psychological separateness.

WORKING OUTSIDE THERAPY

There is also concern that a client can be "therapized" to death. It is important for you to experience life as more than therapy. Abreactive work must be done, but do it in therapy sessions and spend the rest of your time doing something else. Doing abreactive work at home gives abusive alters license to cause you pain. You may feel as if you are doing therapeutic work, but you will fail to integrate the memories and will exhaust your precious emotional resources. If MPD could be cured by home abreactions, there would be no MPD. Every multiple would have been self-cured years ago. Most MPD clients are driven into therapy by a flood of intrusive memories. The recovery of memories alone does not heal multiple personality disorder. Simple memory retrieval is likely to make you more ill by leaving your personality system retraumatized and more chaotic. Give yourself time. The old proverb "You can't push the river" is true for MPD therapy. In this work slower is faster.

You will learn how to do voluntary switching. You will discover how to discuss issues and negotiate with other alters in the system. You will each create a unique safe place in the mind where you can rest, restore yourself and hide from memories that you are not yet ready to assimilate. You will learn how to shut down untimely abreactions. For instance, if you are a salesperson, you cannot be abreacting childhood trauma while waiting on a customer. There will be periods when it seems as if everything causes abreactions, but with time and practice it gets easier.

RELATIONSHIPS AMONG ALTERS

Certain alters will need to stop abusing others. They should make an agreement to stay out of the way of one another when one alter or group of alters is working in the therapy session. Without internal cooperation one alter might block the process in the middle of the therapeutic abreaction of another. Each alter must treat the others in the way he or she wishes to be treated.

There is a natural progression in the relationship among the alters:

1. The alters learn about one another and learn to recognize one another.
2. The alters learn to negotiate with one another, even if there is mutual dislike.
3. The alters learn to cooperate with one another for the common good.
4. The alters appreciate and take care of one another.
5. The alters come to love one another and recognize that they are part of one another.
6. The alters join forces.

Somewhere between learning to cooperate for the common good and learning to appreciate and care for one another, the alters will be ready to help one another share their traumatic recollections. When you and your therapist are confident that the system is ready and has developed enough strength to do the memory work effectively, treatment will focus part of the time on your posttraumatic stress problems through therapeutic abreactions. A therapeutic abreaction integrates the cognitive, emotional, behavioral and physical aspects of the memory and brings all these missing pieces of memory to consciousness in a controlled way. Frank Putnam declares: "Virtually all of the MPD treatment plans published to date deliberately delay the processing of traumata until well into treatment (read years!) and only after other therapeutic interventions have built an alliance and facilitated a measure of internal communication and cooperation." When properly prepared, you will reclaim your traumatic memories. The alters have bits and pieces, but no single personality has integrated and assimilated all the horrific experiences.

Bennett Braun developed the BASK model for dissociated memories. Every memory has four parts: (1) the actual Behaviors; (2) the Affect or emotions associated with the event; (3) the physical Sensations experienced in the trauma and (4) the Knowledge and meaning of what happened. All these parts must be pulled together before the total memory can be assimilated into the self.

If you have accomplished the mastery work, the abreactions can be handled a little at a time: the trickle of a faucet is preferable to the breaking of the dam. Alters can be used to shore up one another, and the process can be completed without the whole system going into meltdown. If you hold a job or have family responsibilities, you should be able to complete therapy and function effectively, *if you do the mastery work first.*

FUSION

As therapy proceeds, the alter parts may form an alliance, share their complementary talents and help one another. Two close personalities may experiment in a temporary blending. Deliberate blending can be used during therapy to help them accomplish a specific task, and some of the alters may fuse spontaneously. In fusion, all that was part of one becomes part of the other and vice versa.

There is a joining of the memories, thoughts, feelings and behaviors, so that nothing is lost. Spontaneous fusions are welcomed as they happen, as long as they do not represent an attempt to seal off the processing of painful memories.

After most of the dissociated memories have been reclaimed by you and all parts of yourself so that there is one common memory, you will no longer have a need for internal secrecy and separateness. The system will have learned that its survival is no longer threatened, that the abuse happened long ago and that the system is now able to care for itself. The remaining alters, fused and singular, come to understand, through observation and experience, that they will be more productive, clearer in perception and more self-directed when integrated. At that time — and only when everyone is ready — the final integrations will happen, marking the end of a long process of internal fusions. A special ceremony during therapy can both facilitate and formally recognize the unification process that has been occurring throughout therapy. It is important to stress that no part of yourself dies off or is lost in the process. Your alter parts will have become like the ego states common to most people. Integration is the formal coming together of your parts to form a new, complex, stronger and more resourceful *you*.

It is possible that your system may want to maintain its alters in a state less defended than MPD alters, but still unintegrated, perceived as other than self. If amnesic barriers remain between alters, however, decision-making will be a problem because there will always be missing data. Important information will be held by alters who will not share it. Without all your data, you will tend to make poor decisions and, sadly, you will be at risk for revictimization. Even with nonamnesic but strongly defended alters, any course of action will require endless negotiation. The system may choose either integration or an executive committee of alters, but integration is the better course.

A real integration must last a minimum of three months to be trusted. Individual alters will no longer be reachable by hypnosis, and the client will no longer hear separate voices inside. Authorities in the field warn that first fusions often do not last. Sometimes first fusions represent a "flight into health" and are effected to please the therapist or to escape further exploration of memories.

POSTFUSION THERAPY

If your integration is real and holds, the next part of therapy is postfusion therapy, for integration is only part of the total treatment process, not the end of it. You must learn how to function in the world as a single and newly formed personality, though it can be very confusing and bewildering. Typically, individuals who forego postfusion therapy will find themselves becoming MPD again. As a rule, this last stage of therapy should last about a year and may involve weekly visits rather than two or three sessions a week.

Therapy for MPD is not mysterious or esoteric. Each year brings a clearer understanding of the process. Effective work with multiplicity is probably more adequately described than work in any other form of psychotherapy.

It is crucial for you to find a knowledgeable therapist you can trust so that you can get started on your journey to wholeness.

S E V E N

The Legend Of The Ektena

A Cherokee Legend

The Legend Of The Ektena is a traditional Cherokee story. You might read this ancient legend out loud so that the internal children can enjoy it. It has an important message.

A long time ago,
    a long, long time ago,
        long before the White Man
        came to this land,
The Cherokee and the Shawnee
    were mortal enemies.

One day a small war party of Shawnee
    invaded Cherokee lands
        and were captured.

The Cherokee warriors
    killed all the Shawnee but one man,
    whom they recognized
        as a very powerful medicine man.

They bound and brought him
    to their mountain village
        and prepared to torture him.

The ancient Cherokee loved
    to test the courage
        of captured enemies by torture.

If the enemy cried out,
    the Cherokee could say,
        "He was not a real man."

If he died silently
    and courageously,
        the Cherokee could take pride
            in beating a worthy opponent.

When the Shawnee medicine man
    was brought into the village,
        he made them an interesting offer.

He said that he knew about
    the great and terrible monster
    that dwelt in the high passes
        of the Smoky Mountains.

This dragon-like monster
    was called Ektena
        and was so terrible
            that even a glance from his flaming eyes
                would kill a warrior
                who stumbled into his presence.

Of course, all Cherokee
    knew of the Ektena.

They remembered that this monster
    had once been a powerful
        Cherokee warrior

back in the days when Grandmother Sun
    had turned against the Cherokee
        and sent horrible fevers to the people.

Back in the days when
    every family was in grief
        as they buried first one
            and then another family member
    until they feared that all the Cherokee
    would die,

When it seemed hopeless,
    the Little People came to rescue them
        by choosing two of the greatest Cherokee
        warriors.

One was magically turned
    into a gigantic rattlesnake, and
    the other was made into the fearsome Ektena.

Now the Ektena had a body
    somewhat similar to a snake's,
        but thicker around than a great tree.

It had horns,
    a blazing crest on its forehead,
        and glittering scales down its side.

Its breath was poisonous,
    its attitude mean,
        and its purpose was
            to kill.

There was no love,
    pride or tenderness left
        in this once proud warrior
        turned killer.

The only place Ektena was vulnerable
  was just below its seventh scale,
    behind which hid its heart
     and its life.

Only one defense held
  against the Ektena;
    neither its body nor its poison
     could pass through fire.

The Ektena was created perfectly
  to do the job
    that the Little People intended.

These two would-be saviors of the people,
  The Giant Rattlesnake
    and the Ektena,
  were instructed to ascend into the sky
    and hide beside the lodge
      of Grandmother Sun's daughter.

Her lodge stood at the noonday point
  in the sky.

Some day, if you watch the sun
  make its journey across the sky,
  you will see that it seems to hang
    at the apex
    for a long time.

People today call this
  High Noon.

The Cherokee believed that the Grandmother
  spent the noon hour
    with her daughter.

So the two protectors,
  the Great Rattlesnake

and the awesome Ektena,
  did as they were told.

They hid patiently beside the lodge
  and prepared for Grandmother Sun
    to approach.

When at last she came close,
  the Great Rattlesnake struck, but
    was so dazzled by her brilliance
    that he missed,
  and hit her daughter by mistake.
    (What happened to her daughter is a whole
      other story).

The two protectors returned to earth
  dejected and ashamed.

The more the Ektena brooded
  about his failure,
  the more humiliated,
    bitter and angry he became,
    until he turned
      against his own people,
      the Cherokee.

At that point the Cherokee conjurors
  banished him
    to the high elevations
      of the Great Smokies,
  where he became a feared killer
    of the people.

The Shawnee magician,
  who knew all about Ektena,
    told the people that
    if they spared his life,
  he would go alone to the mountains
    and destroy the killer.

He also promised
    that he would give the Cherokee
        a great gift
            from the monster.

Now the Cherokee thought,
    "This might be more fun
        than testing him by torture.
    Who knows what the Ektena
        will do to him?"
    And so they accepted
        the Shawnee's offer.

The next morning, the Shawnee
    made his way toward
        the mountains on the northern border
            of Cherokee country.

When he reached the first high pass,
    his way was blocked
        by a black snake as large
            as a pine tree.

The Shawnee stared directly
    into its eyes,
        and walked by.

The Cherokees watching from a distance,
    raised their eyebrows.

Moving South to the next high gap,
    a moccasin snake,
        the largest ever seen,
            lay coiled in his path.

When the people wondered at it,
    he said it was nothing
        and walked on by.

"Humph!"
    said the watching Cherokee.

The next great mountain pass
    was guarded by a huge copperhead,
        as thick as an ancient oak.

The medicine man glared at him,
    spat on the ground,
        and continued his journey.

The Cherokee were impressed,
    to say the least.

Finally, at Gahuti Mountain
    the Medicine Man spied
        the gigantic Ektena,
            coiled asleep.

The Cherokee stayed well back
    out of the way
        as the Shawnee ran
        down the mountain where
he gathered a great circle
    of pine cones.

In the middle of the circle
    he dug a very large trench.

Then he set the pine cones
    on fire.

Quietly he worked his way
    back up the mountain until
        he was within arrow distance
           of the monster.

Carefully scanning the side
    of the sleeping giant,
        he found the seventh scale,
        notched his arrow and
            let it fly
                true to its mark.

Mortally wounded, the Ektena rose
    from its slumber,
    spewing its black blood
        and poisonous breath
            in all directions,
    and began to roll
        down the mountain,
    trees and boulders plunging with it
        as it went.

The medicine man raced downhill,
    jumped through the wall of fire
        and hid on the opposite side
            of the trench.

The monster died at the edge of the fire,
    and his black blood
        filled the trench.

It was said that the women
    for years thereafter
        used the blood
            as a black dye.

The people came closer
    to see the carnage and
        were surprised to hear
    the medicine man calling
        all the bird nations to come
            to eat the corpse.

Birds of all kinds came and
      fed for seven days.

The morning of the eighth day,
      the Shawnee and all the Cherokee
            went back to the scene.

Nothing was left
      but bones.

The medicine man began to search
      the entire area
            for one specific thing.

He searched
      and searched
            until he finally found it,
                  under a bush
                  where it had been dropped
                        by a crow.

Reaching down, he carefully picked up
      a beautiful crystal,
            the source of the crescent light
                  in the Ektena's forehead.

He held it up
      for the people to see,
            and told them that the crystal
                  could be used for powerful healing,
            so long as the Cherokee honored it
                  as the gift of the Ektena.

He told them how to protect,
      store
            and use it forever.

The old ones say that the Ektena's crystal
      is the father of all the crystals

used by healers today,
and it is kept in a special cave
down in the Great Smokies
even as you read this story.

That is the end of the legend of Ektena.

The Ektena legend could also be called the legend of multiple personality disorder. The dragon began as a great warrior determined to protect the people. Failing that, he became a terrible persecutor of the Cherokee. An outsider came, killed the dragon and restored him to his rightful place as a protector and healer of the nation. A stranger and a persecutor became saviors of the Cherokee.

This may be your legend, too, because you probably have alters inside who first came to protect you. Overwhelmed, they became internal dragons or persecutors who may have tried to hurt you. With the help of your medicine man, your inner dragons can find their rightful place again as protectors and helpers.

The big difference in the Ektena legend and your own dragon story is that the Ektena had to be killed before he could give his healing gift to the people. Your dragons will not be harmed. They will be honored and restored to their special place in your personality system.

EIGHT

The Personality System

Most clients are bewildered to find a whole group of personalities sharing their bodies and periodically taking over consciousness. Once aware of their alter personalities, clients often enter into a period of confusion and inner chaos, and it may take a while for the system to settle down to a more comfortable inner coexistence.

Underline the word *system*. It implies relationship, meaning and order, although the order may be difficult to detect. Each of your parts was created for a specific purpose. Just as change is the nature of the universe, so may alters shift and change somewhat in their emphasis while continuing to function within the system.

Some alters exist to hold the pain, to carry painful memories. These are most often child alters who came into being during times of terror and torture when you were overwhelmed. Sometimes, when a child alter first emerges, you will feel that child's terror for the first time. Such experiences may contribute to the chaos that often emerges during the early mapping phases of therapy.

Fierceness and childish rage are the properties of other alters. The child dared not express the anger he or she felt toward the abusers; so the rage was split off and contained by alter personalities who would be protectors for the system as the body grew into adulthood.

Sometimes those very protectors became so frustrated, helpless and angry that they turned their anger inward and became internal persecutors. That is why, so often, there are alters who seem intent on hurting, terrorizing and even destroying the system and the body.

These designated protectors are like the Ektena who was not able to do his job and, in bitter disappointment, became a persecutor. Yet, miraculously, the healing "crystal" of protection is still there within that hidden part, ready to be found. All things change, and persecutors can resume their role as protectors and use their rage in effective ways. The Ektena story is a good illustration of how a gift can be given, lost and regained.

Alter personalities may have other roles as well. For example, one may be an executive, able to organize effectively. Such an alter is a wonderful asset if your job requires organizational and administrative ability.

It is always good to have an Internal Self-Helper who can stand apart from the other alters and make suggestions and observations to facilitate the therapy. During those times when there seems to be no therapeutic progress, such a helper can be a valuable adviser.

Often an alter has promiscuous tendencies and may occasionally involve the body in unplanned and unwise relationships. This can be very distressing for the host and the child alters, who are often rather asexual. After all, you might expect that being sexually abused as a child would make you wary of sexual contact. If you experience overwhelming sexual urges, or unwittingly find yourself in compromising sexual situations, this may be the work of an alter who was sexualized as a child and learned that being sexual was a way to get attention or to mitigate abuse. Once again, all things change and this alter can grow in self-control and the expression of healthy sexuality.

There is no end to the roles that your parts play within the system. There are mother alters, male and female alters, child and adolescent alters, and adult alters. Often there are substance abusers and alters with eating disorders. Some are spiritual, and some may hate spirituality. There may even be animal and demon alters. It is important to remember that each one has a purpose, and the goal is for each to cooperate and join the team while meeting his or her own needs in a way that is helpful to the system.

Just as individual alters have a meaning and purpose, patterns of relationships among them also have specific functions. This may be hard for you to accept when you are feeling so chaotic, but when you can believe that there is order within the confusion, your therapy will have taken another step forward.

The internal system usually reflects one of three structural patterns. The first pattern resembles a tree — major branches stemming from a single trunk as the "primary" personality splits under the pressure of torture, pain and terror. Typically the original split produces three branches or new personalities. Each of these branches may split into other personalities. It is possible, then, to work back down the branches toward the original trunk.

A word of caution: the tree analogy implies that the child had developed a unified personality prior to the first split, whereas in actuality an infant is a collection of ego states. Babies can switch quickly and easily from tears of despair to laughter to wails of frustration because they have not developed the organizing ego of a unified personality. MPD begins during this early phase of development and prevents the maturation of a unified personality. It is a fruitless task to search for the primary or original personality; there probably never was one. The metaphor of a tree adequately describes one of the typical MPD system structures so long as you hold the analogy loosely.

A second pattern of organization resembles an onion. In therapy the client may access a group of alters and then find a second group in a layer below the first. There may

be another group below the second layer; so therapy is a
process of peeling down through the layers. Integration
may come a layer at a time. Occasionally, just when the
therapist and client believe that the whole system is
known, another layer surfaces. Then there is nothing to
do but patiently continue the processes of discovery and
assimilation.

A third pattern of organization resembles a system of
families in which there are adults, adolescents and children. Sometimes they may share the same last name. Communication within the family is usually easy. The task is
to promote communication among families and to build
an internal community of mutual support. Once this is
done, the system will have garnered all its strength for
the work of remembering.

Your structure may or may not be like the ones above.
Perhaps your parts are unrelated to one another and are
all equally accessible to you and your therapist. The truth
is that your way of structuring your selves was perfect
for you. It is also true that, in spite of all the chaos,
confusion and internal warfare, meaningful structures are
in place. Successful therapy will require your inner parts
to work together in positive and harmonious ways.

Memories

Memories! That is what MPD is all about, isn't it? Terrifying memories that flash out of nowhere. Dreams that are more than dreams; dreams so vivid that they "have to be" real. MPD is about recollections that dare not be recalled; a child's experience so traumatic that it had to be dissociated and carried by an alter personality. We are talking about memories so frightening, so ugly, so disgusting that they have been buried, never intended to be exhumed. Yet the feelings remain; the inexplicable terror, and the insistent body pains that do not arise from a physical source.

Memories will probably be the greatest source of shame, confusion, fear, frustration, accomplishment and triumph that you will face during your therapy. The multiple personality system was born to split off and hide memories; so in the early phases of therapy, alters are usually amnesic of one another, each one holding secret his or her trauma. Creating internal parts to hold your secrets was the way you protected yourself from memories you feared would overwhelm you.

The suppression of childhood traumatic memories has been compared to holding a hundred Ping Pong balls under water with your bare hands. It can't be done. Once one ball breaks free and pops to the surface, another is soon to follow. The more you thrash around trying to control the balls, the more certainly you will fail. In much the same way, a system of alter personalities may struggle to hold traumatic memories under the water of the unconscious, only to find the memories breaking free and terrifying you with unexpected and unwanted flashbacks.

How difficult it is to make sense of horrible memory fragments that seem to come from nowhere, memories so repugnant that they require denial. Denial, however, is hard to maintain when flashbacks flood the system with powerful, disruptive emotions.

Flashbacks may be very frightening, especially when you are first becoming acquainted with the presence of alters. Your logical mind tries hard to make sense of the fragmented memories and may attempt to view your recollections as unreal. Yet the body knows what the mind tries vainly to deny. How much can you believe? Are the memories true? Might they be tall tales fabricated by the unconscious for some hidden purpose? You and your therapist will undoubtedly work on these issues many times.

Keep in mind this general guideline: All your memories are to be honored. Each memory that is shared with you has been held and protected by an alter for many years at great emotional price.

You may find that several alters remember the same event. If the experience was unusually traumatic or prolonged, no single personality could encompass it all: others had to share the pain. Usually there are obvious differences between versions of the event. Admitting these inconsistencies can produce confusion, embarrassment and shame because people with MPD commonly have a long history of being labeled liars and troublemakers. You may be overwhelmed, shamed and disgusted enough to seize upon the discrepancies and discount all versions as untrue. Fortunately, denial is not easy.

It is important to understand that no memory is totally accurate. One of the headaches of police work is that witnesses give totally different accounts of the same situation. Memory of what happened is never objective because the event is embedded in subjective meaning.

A three-year-old who witnesses a traumatic event ascribes a three-year-old's understanding and meaning to it. A twelve-year-old will construe the same situation differently, and a thirty-year-old differently again. An event seen by three different individuals will carry three different descriptions based on the individuals' system of meaning and cognitive constructions.

A three-year-old being sexually tortured by her father might describe him as a "monster" or "dragon," because a three-year-old could not "see" her father doing such a thing. An older child might very well perceive the father as capable of torture. The same perceptual processes occur within a multiple personality system. Each alter will perceive an event in a way consistent with his or her age, purpose and abuse history.

The brain struggles valiantly to make meaning out of sights, sounds, smells, touch and impressions, all those things involved in creating an experience. When something happens to a preverbal child, one so young that she does not have words with which to process the experience, the brain finds it even more difficult to shape the sensations into a meaningful, coherent happening. It will search in all directions for an image, metaphor, symbol or other organizing tool. If the client is a member of a trauma group in which she hears the stories of other victims, or if she reads a book about trauma victims, her mind, which is trying so hard to make sense of things, may seize upon metaphors of the other victims and use them.

So what is the objective truth? Is she making something up? Is she seeing monsters in the closet when there was nothing there but the shadows of her dollies? Not at all. The truth is that the child experienced unbelievable trauma, but she may have had to borrow clothing for her memories to make them comprehensible. The truth was the traumatic event. The metaphor was simply a tool used to make understanding possible.

Some people believe that a memory facilitated by hypnosis is more accurate than ordinary memory. It is true that hypnosis usually makes it easier to locate and unfold a memory, but hypnotically induced memories are probably no more accurate than any other kind. While hypnosis is the standard and best tool for getting to know a personality system, it does not guarantee accuracy in recall. Putnam declares:

> The veracity of memories recovered by hypnosis or while the patient is in a drug-facilitated twilight state of consciousness is of primary concern in the clinical application of these techniques. Frequently, clinicians inexperienced in this area believe that the memories and affects produced by the abreactive reliving of events in an altered state of consciousness are true and valid representations of those past events. This is not necessarily the case. Serious therapeutic complications can arise if the therapist and client unquestioningly regard such memories as the whole truth and nothing but the truth. Research has shown that pseudomemories can be suggested under these conditions and that these false memories may be experienced by the subject as genuine recollections of past experiences. Confabulation can occur.

Amytal is less widely used than hypnosis because it provides no more accuracy and carries the possibility of negative side effects. Nancy Hornstein, a researcher and consultant in child and adult dissociative disorders is very reluctant to use Amytal interviews for the recovery of traumatic memories because of the invasive medical nature of the technique. The safe use of Amytal requires admission to a hospital or a facility that has an anesthesiologist present who can assist the patient's breathing if he or she becomes too sedated. An intravenous catheter must be inserted into a vein to administer the Amytal, and the patient needs time to recover from the effects of the drug following the procedure. Your personality system would probably experience this procedure as additional abuse.

So what *may* be believed? We are back to the original dilemma. Honor each memory as a gift, offered at great sacrifice. Whether or not one set of memories agrees with another, honor all of them; do not carve them in granite however. No matter how strange a memory may be, neither discount it nor accept it as the final version.

It is helpful to find corroborating evidence whenever and wherever possible. You may have siblings or relatives who saw the abuse or who were abused as well. Sometimes school records will suggest abuse. Medical records are certainly a place one might check. Some clients have found photographs that clearly show the abuse. While concrete evidence can be very upsetting, it also gives credence to the testimony of the alter personalities.

Every little piece of hard data you can collect will help you remember and accept what has happened to you. Even though details of memories may differ and your parts may argue with one another, you will become more and more confident that you will ultimately know the whole truth about what has happened to you.

You may be wondering impatiently, "When will I know the truth? When will all these memory fragments come together to complete the story? When will I know that I have it all?" Neither this book nor your therapist can predict when all the "telling" will be finished and your history will be unified, coherent and complete. You will know that you have finished integrating a memory when it no longer haunts you or causes much emotional reaction in you.

Your therapy will take time, but once all the alter personalities have told their stories you will have a much more accurate grasp of your past. The *meaning* of your past experiences will be much clearer after all your parts are integrated and the various perceptions of your traumas have merged into a single perception.

Certain physical symptoms and sensations often signal emerging memories. Although very unpleasant, these physical experiences may be a good sign that your therapy is working:

- excessive vaginal bleeding
- excessive nasal bleeding
- persistent joint pain
- genital and/or rectal pain
- sore throat
- earache, eye pain, visual blurring, inability to open eyes
- pseudoseizures
- dizziness
- hearing sounds or sudden deafness
- flu-like vomiting
- excessive sleepiness
- recurring smells
- partial body anesthesias
- aching pain in upper arms
- stomach bloating, pain
- gagging, feelings of suffocation
- headaches
- very hot or cold skin
- eating disorders.

Any one of the symptoms, of course, may result from infection or other disorder, but these symptoms are extremely common in the course of MPD treatment; they are often body memories trying to surface. You must make sure that you have no underlying physical problem. If you are medically cleared, your body pain may lead you to the other parts of the traumatic memory. Remember the BASK model discussed in Chapter 6? Physical discomfort is the sensation part of the memory, and it must be integrated with the behavior, affect and knowledge parts of the experience.

Until you have been integrated for at least six months, it would be best to refrain from public disclosure of your memories. Your recollections are personal and private and should not be subjected to the humiliating scrutiny of outsiders. It is sad to watch an individual with MPD go into court prematurely and level charges at his or her abusers. It almost always goes badly because a clever defense attorney can find the inconsistencies and variances that routinely exist between the alters, and the individual ends up looking like a cross between a liar and a "mental case."

For the same reason, it is usually a poor idea to go on a TV or radio show before therapy is finished. You will not have all your data together. Your memories will not yet have gone through the leavening process of having all the alters work through the discrepancies. Be patient. If you complete your work before you go public, your testimony will reflect the power of your whole personality.

Be patient with the therapy process as well. Give yourself time. It may be very confusing now, and what you are remembering may appear to be patently crazy, but wait and see. Let the alters give their testimony. Gather all the corroborating evidence you can. Integrate. Then you will have one set of unified memories. Knowing your history, you can effectively face the present and plan for the future.

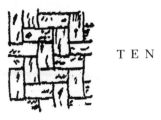

Shame

Shame is like summer humidity for the multiple. It is always there, inescapable. Like the atmosphere, it envelops you, smothers you, drowns you in its essence. Shame is so pervasive in the background of daily existence that it is felt rather than recognized. The continual struggle to repress it may seriously deplete the life energy contained within the MPD system.

There is a plethora of written material about shame. The Recovery Movement alerts us to shame's power and ubiquity among abuse survivors. Each writer speaks differently about the subject, and there is no consensus about its nature or the differences between shame and guilt. Often the two words are used interchangeably.

Donald Nathanson has provided a framework for understanding all the emotions, especially shame, in both their physiological and their psychological aspects. Nathanson has explored the difference between the physical reactions and sensations of shame and the intellectual explanation we give ourselves for being ashamed. He has shown that although the physical shame response is very clear, one may be completely mistaken about why it is being experienced. In other words, when asked, "Why are you so ashamed?" you may not know or may give the wrong reason.

A thorough explanation of Nathanson's work is beyond the scope of this chapter, but it is helpful to have at least a fair understanding of the nature of emotion. When an emotion overtakes us, we are primarily aware of the subjective experience of it — the dread, fear, leadenness or euphoria. Secondarily we may notice that we are sweating, being chilled or feeling numb. Nathanson, building on the work of Silvan Tomkins, describes the three primary components of what we call an emotion.

Nathanson compares the emotion to a computer that has three necessary parts: the hardware, the firmware and the software. The hardware consists of the box and electronic connections, the machine part. The firmware consists of the internal chip that tells the machine what language to use: for example, C++. The software consists of the programs we put into our machine to make it do what we want — word processing, spreadsheet or database.

In the human being the *hardware* is made up of the physical body, the nervous system and the various chemical systems. The *firmware* consists of those innate programs, common to all of us, that are directly related to our drives and affects. If we are startled, there is a universal physical reaction. Fear has its own specific physical response, as does shame. *Software* consists of those learned programs by which we cope with life: for example, one small piece of shame software that tells us that we do not go nude into public places.

The emotion of shame is expressed through the following events. It begins with a specific environmental trigger — a certain look, tone of voice or gesture directed at you. Your brain makes an instant interpretation — "Be ashamed!" — and your body responds appropriately. Your neck muscles relax, letting the head droop and turn aside. Your eyes avert, and the veins in the neck and face dilate to create a blush. You become instantly aware of the intense physiological feelings and begin to search for an explanation. You need to know why you are having a shame attack. The problem is that the physical feelings of shame must be understood in terms of past shame experiences. There is no other possible way to understand them, and so you search your shame memory files until you find an immediate explanation: for instance, "I am ashamed because I am worthless today (just as I was when I was being abused and felt really shameful)." That self-message, which you use to account for the current discomfort, may not be related at all to the trigger for this particular shame attack. All shame responses have exactly the same physical components; the only variance will be why the shame is felt. As we shall see later, it is extremely important for survivors to examine the "why" messages.

The physiological shame response is encoded in the brain of every human being. It is there at birth just waiting to be used. By three months of age, the infant begins to activate the shame program. The newborn works full time — every waking moment — at trying to understand and control his or her environment. I had a colleague once who affixed a string to the foot of his infant daughter and connected the string to a mobile. The baby soon learned that moving her foot would cause the mobile to swing. She took obvious delight in controlling that small part of her world. If the string was removed from one foot and attached to the other, the baby quickly switched feet to swing the mobile.

The baby's ability to communicate with mother is crucial for survival. Since language develops much later, the infant communicates by pairing facial expressions with mother and shows delight when her smile is reflected by her mother's smile. But what happens when mother comes to change a dirty diaper? Baby smiles up at her, and, instead of receiving a mirroring smile back, the baby sees a disgusted face or an angry face or a withholding, blank face. The baby immediately shows the physiological shame response: the head droops and turns away, eyes avert and there may be an obvious blush. These physical signs, first seen at about three months of age, will signal shame throughout life, regardless of race or culture.

Every time the infant fails to accomplish what she has been able to do previously, she will show the shame response triggered by an experience of failure. Shame does not require an interpersonal situation. A baby who has learned to control the flashing of colored lights will show all the signs of shame upon finding that the lights no longer respond to her movements. In that moment she experiences failure. If the infant had words, she might describe herself as confused, mute and unable to focus. When the physical shame affect is perceived, the brain instantly shuts down all responses while it searches the memory bank for an appropriate explanation of why it happened. When an adult has this physical response, she immediately checks her memory bank for similar situations. She may come up with the memory of being called clumsy or dumb, and will say, "I feel shame because I am a stupid klutz." Yet the trigger for this particular shame response may have been unrelated to her grace or intelligence.

Incest survivors make a very common mistake that illustrates the point. A father, intent on sexually molesting his daughter, might have begun by saying, "You are very pretty tonight." The youngster, internalizing shame about the incest, might confuse being called pretty with being sexually dirty. Years later, upon receiving a compliment from her boyfriend, she immediately feels ashamed. The young woman might then tell herself, "I am too dressed up, too noticeable." Her interpretation of the shame feelings focuses on the way she is dressed, when actually the shame has to do with her father and incest. The current shame attack was triggered by an innocent compliment from her boyfriend.

SHAME AND THE INDIVIDUAL

From early infancy each of us has built up a library of shame/failure experiences; and each time the physiological shame response is triggered, we try to understand it by comparisons in our memory file. It is important to remember this, for it will regularly affect your MPD therapy.

Shame plays a positive role in human development. Parents strive to instill appropriate behaviors in their children. "Johnny, do not pick your nose in public. I know you think it is terribly funny to flip boogers, but it is not nice. Now, stop it!" The mandates go on and on. You know all of them. When Johnny is grown, should he be caught surreptitiously flipping a booger, he will experience momentary shame. That is an example of positive shame. It helps us behave in a civilized, culturally approved manner.

Toxic shame, to use Bradshaw's term, is the shame that destroys the sense of self-worth. When a father sexually uses his daughter and then crudely tells her she "wanted it" and is a slut and a whore whom no decent person would ever want, he is dumping a load of toxic shame on her. She will carry that pain forever and believe what he said about her because he was her father and he should know. Her personal boundaries were not strong enough to hold his toxic messages at bay. As Bradshaw says, every child survivor carries shame that rightfully belongs to the abuser. Because the abuser was shameless the child absorbed the abuser's message and believed it. Toxic shame strikes at the very core of the beliefs we hold about ourselves.

Each time the child is abused, her load of shame grows until it becomes an unbearable burden. Considering that the typical survivor with MPD had multiple abusers over a long period of time, it is no wonder that shame is such a pervasive, negative force in her life.

Shame is found in the presence of other strong emotions such as fear, anger, depression and even joy, but it is most often identified with guilt. Many writers confuse shame and feelings of guilt, which are related but not the same. Feelings of guilt emerge when you know that you have violated rules of conduct and behavior. Arising from the violation of values, it may condemn you when you have hurt or behaved hurtfully toward another person. It is resolved when you make amends or take your punishment. You do it; you pay for it; and it is finished. Shame is that internal pain we feel when we recognize our own defects. It is more than just having violated a rule. It is the exposure, either outwardly or inwardly, of our unworthiness. It cannot be eradicated by punishment or erased by good behavior.

Toxic shame is the poison of the self. It enlarges those momentary feelings of failure that all of us experience into weapons against the spirit. Child abuse, whether physical, emotional, sexual or ritual, invariably creates toxic shame in its victim.

As the child is abused, she begins to believe the derogatory messages levied against her. "I deserve what is happening to me." "Anyone like me can't expect more than this." The child may even assist the abusers. After all, she has not been allowed to develop a sense of boundaries. She cannot tell where the perpetrator's emotions leave off and hers begin. From birth she has wanted only to gain some control and mastery over her environment. If control entailed assisting the abusers, that was what she had to do.

Pia Mellody describes how the child with permeable boundaries internalizes the feelings of the perpetrators. Without boundaries the child cannot defend against the incoming feelings of her abusers:

The abuser's anger leads to the child's rage.
The abuser's pain leads to the child's hopelessness and despair.
The abuser's fear leads to the child's panic and paranoia.
The abuser's shamelessness adds to the child's shame and poisons her self-concept.

Once these toxic messages are introjected, they run continuously — like an endless tape loop in the brain. Some have estimated that the normal individual has 25,000 hours of such tapes in his head. In addition, the MPD individual will often have one or more alters as internalized abusers who repetitiously shout derogatory and shaming remarks at her.

People with MPD are so bombarded by internal messages of shame that most of their reactions are colored by them. Their behavioral repertoire of responses can be plotted on the Compass Of Shame as described by Nathanson. Shame manifests itself in one of four ways: avoidance, withdrawal, an attack on the self or an attack on another.

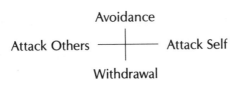

Figure 1. The Compass Of Shame

While the situation may dictate which response is used, the individual develops one more than others and prefers it in most shame-provoked situations. Some people are so wary of shame that they avoid any situation in which a shame attack might be triggered. They use the avoidance mode, and their continual wariness produces massive resistance in therapy.

Who has not had the experience of being embarrassed and wanting nothing more than to get out of the situation at all costs? "I was so embarrassed I just wanted to die" is the sentiment of a person using withdrawal.

The attack-others mode is used by MPD individuals who have found belligerence to be their safest posture. Their typical response is verbal (sometimes physical) attack. By assailing another and creating interpersonal distance, they seek to hide the shamefulness of the self from public view. The opposite attack mode, expressed in self-mutilation, substance abuse and suicide, turns the aggression in upon the self, causing more shame and lowered self-esteem.

I have watched my clients struggle with the withdrawal/avoidance blocks that shame has erected in their therapy. I have felt the heat of their verbal attacks as they have defended themselves against the awfulness of their memories, and I have watched with apprehension as they have struggled with alters that want to end the pain by suicide.

I have felt my own rage at those perpetrators who have callously dumped such a heavy load of shame on my clients. In therapy the question emerges, "How do we purge the library of shame memories so that you experience only the shame that belongs to you?"

Bradshaw tells the parable of a man who was sentenced to die and was imprisoned in a totally dark cave. He was told that there was a way of escape if he could find it, and that if he escaped, it would prove his innocence. He was further warned that he would be provided bread and water for thirty days, no longer.

The man, realizing that his time was limited, began to consider all possible ways of escape. It soon became apparent to him that the only way out was through the tiny opening in the roof of the cave through which his food and water were provided. The opening, however, was about eighteen feet above his head. To reach the opening he would have to arrange a pile of dirt and stones at least twelve feet high. He began to spend all his waking hours crawling around the cave, gathering rocks, digging up dirt and building his tower to freedom.

As the days passed, he realized he would have to work even harder if he was to finish before his food and water were cut off. The frantic struggle coupled with such poor nutrition took its toll, and he became weaker and weaker. Finally the tower was high enough so that he just might be able to reach the opening. When he tried, the stones under his feet slipped, and he fell to the floor of the cave. Exhausted and depleted, he died.

When his captors rolled the stone away from the cave opening and light flooded the interior, a three foot wide opening was exposed on the opposite side of the cave. It was the way to freedom, which had been there all the time, hidden in the dark.

It is crucial for you to extricate yourself from the blackness of old messages of toxic shame. Otherwise you will waste your resources defending against the pain rather than finding the door to your freedom.

THE WAY OUT

The path to freedom from shame is the same path you must follow to wholeness. One of the greatest virtues is patience, patience and more patience. It takes time. The pain is not forever, but it was a long time in building and it will take time to eliminate.

First accept what Pia Mellody calls "your perfect falli-bility." The child believes that the only escape from shame is to be perfect. Sadly, the abuser's world held so many double binds and inconsistencies that, no matter what the child did, it was deemed "wrong" and shameful. Accept the fact that in your life, as an adult, you will make mis-takes and reap the discomfort of normal shame. Mellody puts it graphically when she warns that "Poop smells." Accept the fact that your poop smells, yours and everyone else's. You must discern whether the odor that stifles you belongs to you or to your abuser.

Commit yourself to the mastery work outlined in Chapter 6. Nothing you do in the early stages of therapy is as important as opening communication within and among the parts of your system of alters. Certain alters will carry the toxic shame messages. They are not to be blamed but rather appreciated for their attempt to protect you. We can say they are misguided, but they have done the best they could in their abusive world. It is especially important for you to know them and to enter into internal dialogue with them.

Talk about the shame in therapy. You can take the evil power out of toxic shame by exposing it to the light. The safest place to do that is in your therapist's office. You undoubtedly have a tape that says, "If you let him know your shame, he will be repelled and reject you. If you tell, he will abandon you." Expect to hear that message over and over again. Argue with it because it is not true. If you let shame control you, you will forever be locked in the black cave.

Encourage each alter to share his or her shame with the others and with your therapist. You can facilitate this by keeping a journal in which you write down your experiences, feelings and memories of abuse.

Pay attention to your internal dialogue, and watch out for internal shaming. For instance, survival probably dictated that alters be cooperative and willing participants in abusive sex or ritual practices. Having done what was required, they now carry the toxic shame that rightfully belongs to the perpetrating adults. It is too easy for the other alters to point accusing fingers and denigrate the shamed alters as dirty, filthy, evil and beyond acceptance. Remind yourself that they are you and you are them. You belong together as a system. Their participation in the rituals and sex saved you from having to participate. There is no place for internal shaming.

Practice affirmations of love. Begin to record positive internal tapes that can override some of your persistent negative tapes. An affirmation is a positive statement that you repeat to yourself until it begins to imprint. You might record such statements as these on your positive tapes:

- I am a worthy person.
- I am more and more in control of my life.
- I am more and more open to the power of love in my life.

Write your own affirmations. Make them positive statements: "I *am*" rather than "I am *not*". If you have trouble writing your own, get help from your therapist or go to a "recovery" bookstore where you can find affirmation cards or a small book of affirmations. Suggestion plays a big part in life. It is time to replace negative suggestions with positive ones.

Practice loving behaviors internally. Therapy will help you to go inside and locate your alter personalities. There you will find them carrying on various activities. Some will be afraid or emotionally hurt. Encourage stronger alters to take care of the hurt ones. You have within your system incredible capacities for healing and love as well as the capacity for pain. By encouraging your alters to nurture one another, you will be learning to care for yourself.

Practice assertiveness toward shaming and invasive people. Sadly there are people in your world who will continue to dump shame on you when they can. It is a sign of their own sickness. They will also invade your boundaries because they do not know their own. When you are invaded, it raises all the old messages of toxic shame: "I am a bad person if I say no." You have alters who are perfectly capable of defending you if you will let them. You also may have alters who would be violent rather than assertive; so let them out carefully, making sure that the system stays in control. It is not appropriate to shoot field mice with ballistic missiles, but you can tell the intruders and shame-givers to back off. You have every right to do so.

Finally, become alert to individuals and situations that trigger toxic shame in you. Avoid them. Nothing says that you must subject yourself to their poison. This may mean turning away from certain friends or family members if they are bad for you. You are not obligated to remain in a destructive relationship.

Toxic shame forms the background against which all your therapeutic work is performed. The very physiological response of shame blocks your ability to work by confusing your thoughts and rendering you speechless. Recognize it when it comes. Disown the shame that rightfully belongs to your abuser. Then take steps to liberate yourself from it. There is an escape from the cave.

ELEVEN

Family, Friends, Lovers And Careers

An MPD survivor can well describe the cacophony of inner voices competing for control. With so much inner turmoil, it is no wonder that little energy is left for the outside world of family, friends, lovers and career. Yet most multiples have families and friends. Some hold down responsible jobs, and some have an active love life. Clearly the problem is to find a balance between the inner and outer worlds — much easier said than done. Maintaining an internal equilibrium takes so much psychic energy that outside relationships and responsibilities are often neglected. This chapter will examine some of these external relationships.

THE FAMILY OF ORIGIN

Before discovering her multiple personality disorder, the client may have a very starry-eyed view of her parents and siblings. She may initially describe her family as perfect, with a hard-working father, dedicated to his children, and a mother who is always loving and available. Often the family still holds regular holiday reunions as both parents and siblings collude in building the myth of the perfect family. Only after a period of good therapy does the real family picture begin to emerge under the clarifying light of recovered memory.

The truth is that almost every multiple's family of origin was abusive. Fear, pain, degradation and torture severe enough to cause the fragmentation of MPD must have involved the child's family. In those cases in which the parents did not actively engage in the abuse, they were probably guilty of neglect by not sheltering the child from situations in which abuse could occur. It is also true that MPD has been caused by medical and other trauma that was unavoidable; generally, however, the family was directly or indirectly involved in abuse.

Sadly, once the abuse is remembered and the family exposed, the survivor is usually pressured to be silent. Family members may actively attempt to obstruct the therapy. Siblings will threaten to break off relationships. Everyone suffers as the family myth is labeled a lie. Those selfparts of the MPD client who remember only the "good" parents will struggle with alters who demand that the abuse be known. So MPD individuals are torn between their family of origin and their warring internal alter selves.

If you are diagnosed as having multiple personality disorder, your therapist will probably ask whether one of your parents or siblings also has MPD. An individual who could abuse at the level required to produce multiple personality disorder could also have been subjected to extreme childhood abuse and might be MPD. It is not uncommon to find multiple personality disorder in other family members.

If you remain in the abusive home, the abuse may continue into adulthood. Under the roof of perpetrating parents you continue to be vulnerable. Even if you are away from home, the abuse may continue: alters could take your body back for house visits under the cloak of amnesia if those selfparts, long ago, entered into alliances with your abusers. The abuse may even continue indirectly via telephone, with the perpetrators using your cooperative alters to maintain control over you.

It is usually necessary to cut off or severely limit contact with parental perpetrators until all the alter parts are joined in the therapeutic venture. Even then you will continue to be vulnerable and will experience severe stress if you have more than superficial contact with those who abused you. Expect alters committed to the family to be deeply grieved, even if they realize the necessity of breaking family contact.

Sibling relationships can be problematic for several reasons. Brothers and sisters may be deeply in denial. Though recognizing their amnesia for childhood and adolescent years, they may be equally determined to remember nothing. In that case you will be called a liar and destroyer of the family. You may experience extreme pressure to shut up or to recant. You can only hope that someday they, too, will wake up.

Suppose, however, that some of your siblings are in therapy and working through their own problems. How much do you share of your memories? If you are aware of any danger to a sibling, you should protect him or her but if you find you share memories, it is good to confirm and be confirmed in the recollections. It would be better not to volunteer new memories until your sibling is well along into his or her therapy. Research clearly demonstrates that the memories of one individual can contaminate the memories of another. Let your siblings work individually, and then let the memories be mutually validated.

Once you understand the nature and extent of your abuse, you may experience a great amount of anger at your less abusive parent. For instance, a daughter remembering paternal incest may be more angry at her mother than her father. She may feel betrayed by the mother who did not protect her. As a child she may even have tried to expose the incest to her mother, only to be punished for lying. She may discover that her mother consciously knew of the incest and could not or would not do anything about it.

So what do you do about your abuse and your anger at the perpetrating parents? People will admonish you to forgive your parents and get on with your life. You may feel a religious obligation to forgive, and when you cannot, your shame may condemn you. The truth is that you cannot forgive until you know what needs forgiving. Throwing a blanket of forgiveness over the perpetrators without a clear grasp of your abuse history is about as effective as smothering a bonfire with a bed sheet. It may be a noble idea, but it will not work.

After uncovering your history and the role your parents played in your abuse, you can decide about forgiveness. You may confront them to see if they will face the situation honestly with you. You may determine to have nothing more to do with them but relinquish your burning anger toward them. Or you may decide on a limited relationship. You may even choose to recognize their own victimization and forgive them without forgiving their abusive behavior. You have many options, but you cannot make a legitimate choice until you know your past.

SPOUSE AND CHILDREN

If you have MPD, just saying "Hello" to your spouse and children may evoke such inner responses as, "He's not my husband!" "She's not my wife!" "I don't care who they belong to, but they're not my children!" Although it is a very different constellation from your family of origin, your current family is also full of confusion: the relationships resonate with transferences; the alliances between various alters and family members are often inconsistent and at cross purposes. Your current family may express a pattern of unconscious abuse that negatively affects parents and children, but with understanding and love your family may also become supportive and healing for all its members.

For anyone, the decision to marry is complex and not always based on sound judgments. The MPD individual rarely has the luxury of making an uncomplicated commitment to anything, especially to marriage. There are currents of transference, waves of fear and riptides of co-dependency. Somehow the multiple must float his or her dreams of marriage on a treacherous ocean of opposition-al purposes.

Generally one alter dates the prospective spouse, falls in love and makes the marriage. Some of the child alters may eagerly anticipate marriage, hoping for the father they always wanted. Other alters may be very sexualized and expect continual sexual encounters. Still other inner parts may not like the potential spouse and may reject him at every opportunity.

Let's take a closer look. The husband, for his part, may be playing out his own dysfunctional family themes. If he was a rescuer in his family of origin, he may be replaying that role with his wife's helpless child alters who need his strength. If he felt neglected in his family of origin, his ego may be inflated by the exaggerated attention of his wife's sexualized alters. He might regard this marriage as heaven-sent until reality sets in.

Once the marriage is consummated and the wife's alter selves feel locked into the relationship, she may face inter-nal rebellion. Those parts that have been sexually abused may adamantly reject physical intimacy, thus leaving the husband totally puzzled by the change in his wife's behav-ior. The more independent alters may refuse his desire to nurse his "dependent" wife. Confused, he cannot imagine what has happened.

All parts of the marital relationship are complicated when MPD is present, but no area is more complicated than that of sexual intimacy. In the great majority of cases, the MPD client has been sexually violated many times. Some of the alter parts are highly sexual and de-mand a lot of attention. Other parts are frightened of sex. Once the MPD is discovered and treatment begins, the sexually frightened child parts will probably be more ex-pressive, and marital sex may either be terminated or severely limited.

Upon discovering the partselves in his wife, the husband may learn to trigger the alter he wants at any moment. One husband was reported to boast, "I have a harem and have to pay for only one wife." It is possible for the MPD survivor to be revictimized within her new family.

Periodic marriage counseling may be helpful as an adjunct to MPD therapy. It is especially useful to educate the husband about MPD and to assure him of its treatability. The husband may also have psychological issues that need to be addressed. He may have married an abuse survivor with MPD for some unconscious reason. If the husband is playing out a dysfunctional caretaking role carried over from his family of origin, he may unconsciously try to keep his wife from getting well, but if educated about MPD, he can become an enormous support to her. Truly, as the wife works through her multiplicity and realizes the strength within her personality system, all the family relationships will change. The family is a system in which each member has a role. When the MPD individual begins to change, everyone in the system must change. The family system will typically resist any modification by subverting therapy. With some guidance, education and commitment, the family can become a stable source of support for the health of all its members. Periodic marriage or family counseling should help the family work through the difficult time of MPD therapy and emerge as a strong unit when therapy ends.

The physical children (as opposed to child alters) in the family require special consideration. Unfortunately, they are at special risk for abuse. Some of the MPD alters probably know only abusive ways of relating to children. If these alters have identified with perpetrators, they may compulsively abuse their own children, for children in the family are convenient victims; they must be protected. Having MPD is not tantamount to abusing your children, however. Some MPD survivors do, but many do not. Because the potential is there you must be aware of it and take precautions. It is a good idea to have your children evaluated by an independent therapist early in treatment to make sure that they have not been abused and are safe.

FRIENDS

People with MPD need friends, too. It is good to have friends outside the family with whom you can visit and share time. Part of the therapeutic process is developing your boundaries and knowing your limits. Friendships can provide a living laboratory in which to experiment with limit-setting and intimacy.

If your friends are abuse survivors, and especially if they suffer from a dissociative disorder, it is doubly important for you to hold your boundaries firmly intact because your alter parts, particularly the traumatized child alters, cannot tell where the friends' trauma memories leave off and yours begin. If your time with friends is spent in swapping trauma tales or sharing the latest abreaction, two things are bound to happen: your traumatized child alters will be retraumatized, and everyone's traumatic memories will become so contaminated that it will be nearly impossible to unravel what happened to whom.

In addition, if your friends are MPD survivors, the whole therapeutic process can become contaminated by your treating one another as adjunct therapists. You may find that you spend all your friendship time talking about MPD and then have nothing left for your therapy. Since merely recounting memories does *not* lead to their assimilation, the whole therapeutic process can be delayed.

Positive, negative and traumatic transferences will also play a part in all your friendships, especially friendships with other multiples. Because of your abuse history you need stability around you. You crave predictability. You cannot stand change, and you hate surprises. If your friend is an MPD survivor, you cannot count on stability in the friendship until both of you are well. Just about the time you have a relationship, the other person will change. Although you may understand that she is multiple, your own system does not want to excuse her propensity to switch alter personalities.

If your multiple friend is of the opposite sex, the relationship may be even more traumatic. He will represent all the good and evil in your abusers. Your friend may actually have alter parts that correspond to characteristics of the perpetrators, and you will be caught up in the love-hate-fear responses you felt as an abused child. Opposite-sex friendships are incredibly complicated for MPD individuals.

There are real advantages, though, to having MPD friends. Your friends will understand your up-and-down moods and your changing self-presentations. During crisis times an MPD friend may understand and support you as no one else can. It will be easier for you to maintain these relationships if you remember that your friend is just as multiple as you are. If you have ten alter parts and she has eight, there will be eighty possible relationships between the two of you! Try to make room for her alter selves, and remind your friend to make room for yours. Work at being patient with your friend. The strong intensity of your emotions can be overwhelming and frightening to her, just as her intense feelings can frighten your timid alter selves. Both of you will need to guard your boundaries fiercely.

It is good to include "normals," people who are not abuse survivors or dissociative, among your friends. Sometimes this is difficult because one feels more comfortable among people who are focused on their own psychological issues. There are good and healthy people outside of the Recovery Movement. Include some of them in your circle of friends. Look forward to the day when you will have recovered from MPD. Be open to friendships that will outlive therapy and will be there for you when you are well.

ROMANCE

Romantic involvements may stress anyone, but when MPD individuals begin to date, they will be buffeted by all kinds of reactions. One alter self may be very attracted to an individual; a second alter may be repelled; a third alter may be in a panic; and a fourth alter may be gay or lesbian and offended by any heterosexual relationship. The host, who simply wants to go on a date, may experience all these feelings simultaneously. It is normal for anyone to be ambivalent about a first date. The difference is that most people can process all their feelings together and understand them as a whole. This is not so for the multiple.

Please take this warning very seriously. Revictimization is always a hazard in multiple personality disorder. Some of the alter selves probably know only the victim role. They may have survived by being cooperative objects of abuse. Searching for a perpetrator, they may be attracted to potential victimizers and signal their vulnerability to abuse. Every part of the system must be alert to prevent victim alters from choosing destructive romantic partners. Plenty of people will be respectful of you, but there are also some cruel and manipulative individuals who stalk potential victims. All of your self parts can protect you by sharing information and being cautious. You have the right to healthy relationships, and you can make good choices. You have the internal wisdom. Use it!

Expect more positive, negative and traumatic transferences with your romantic partners than with your friends. When your boyfriend is humanly imperfect, he may seem just like your abusive father. Remind yourself that your boyfriend is *not* your father. Even when your boyfriend is perfect in every way, remind yourself that he is *not* your father. Your male companion is a unique person, neither perfect nor evil, neither your good nor bad father. Your male friend is his own person.

Sex may be an issue from the beginning. Your boyfriend will probably want a physical relationship. Part of you may want it, and part may not. You must negotiate with your child alters, reminding them that the times of abuse are past. Tell them that you want to be with this person, that he is safe for all of you. Should he prove to be unsafe, you will immediately withdraw from him. Assure all your self parts that you can and will protect them. Encourage their withdrawal to prepared "safe places" during sexual times. They need not be involved in sexual activities until they are ready. Shield your child parts and make them feel safe. It goes without saying that if your partner is not respectful, you must protect yourself. Do not participate in even a mildly abusive situation.

As the relationship develops, you will want to share information about your multiplicity. It is surely unwise to begin a relationship by saying, "Hi! My name is Mary, and I am a multiple." You are much more than an individual who has MPD. Remember that everyone has ego states, even your new boyfriend. Your MPD is differentiated from his multiplicity by the amnesia and chaos of your personality system. Your MPD is information to be shared as other personal information is shared. It is not your crucial, defining characteristic. You are infinitely more than an individual with MPD!

EMPLOYMENT

There is a limit to how much physical and psychic energy a single body can retain, especially if it holds multiple personalities. If you have a spouse and children, you may be unable to work outside the home. If you are a single parent, employment may be the only choice for you because of your financial requirements.

If you are single and without children, you should work outside the home if at all possible. Being single and unemployed can mean that the bulk of your psychic energy is tied up in endless struggles among the alters, thus eliminating any life outside your personality system. A regular job will help ground you and structure your day. It will force you to have a life other than being MPD.

Employment will require coordination within your system. There must be internal agreement about which alter selves will go to work. It would be inappropriate for child or adult alters to be abreacting and acting out at work. All these alters are part selves of you, your system. Through negotiation among your parts, you can agree upon which ones will appear at the office.

Many MPD individuals are extraordinarily productive because some of their alters are exclusively task-oriented and experienced in what they do. There are surgeons, nurses, therapists, salespeople and executives who also happen to have MPD. You name the job and multiples have done it well.

At many times during therapy, however, the system is in such chaos that it is difficult to work. Even then the emotions can be calmed and the system quieted until it is safe to process emotions again. Learning to self-soothe is part of therapy. Still, some individuals experience so much internal chaos and terror that they are disabled for employment. There is no shame in that. Therapy can help the personality system become organized so that it can calm the hyper-arousal state and attain a functioning level commensurate with employment.

If you have multiple personality disorder, you know the whole array of interpersonal problems that must be solved by any person, MPD or not. Your problems are exacerbated by the number of discrete part selves in your system, each with its own hopes, dreams, fears and agendas. To withdraw behind the walls of your home is the worst choice you can make. Find friends. Work on boundary issues. Learn to live effectively in the world of human beings. You have more internal resources than you ever imagined.

Brain Work: The Neurochemistry Of MPD

You are excruciatingly aware of how multiple personality disorder feels. You are on intimate terms with terror, rage, shame and numbness. So far, we have focused exclusively on the subjective experience of your disorder. You have recognized that there is meaning and purpose within your personality system. Although you may not understand it, there is order within your chaos.

This chapter will describe in simple terms the complex ways in which your brain has responded to your trauma and you will see that paralleling every emotional response there is an underlying chemical process.

Trauma established patterns of brain responses in ways that were protective of you as a child but now cause you trouble. This parallels the contribution of alter personalities that allowed you to survive childhood trauma but are probably causing the problems associated with MPD as an adult. Your alters were the most effective defense available to you as a child fighting to survive horrendous tortures and abuse, but as an adult you are facing an entirely different set of problems and stresses, and you need to face them with adult resources. In the same way, the trauma-conditioned reactions within your brain have also become counterproductive. Who can say which process is primary: the experience of MPD or the brain's response to trauma? They are two sides of the same coin. Understanding one side will help you to understand the other. This chapter focuses on the neurochemistry of MPD.

PTSD: THE EITHER/OR RESPONSE

MPD is a complex form of posttraumatic stress disorder (PTSD). This is important to know, as much brain research has been focused on PTSD studies of war veterans. Post-traumatic stress, however, is found throughout the population, particularly among survivors of child abuse and torture. It encompasses specific physical and psychological responses to trauma.

Once you have lived through serious trauma, your response to stress thereafter will have two phases: revivification and numbing. In the first phase, you relive the original horror with all its attendant feelings; *revivification* may involve hyperactivity, explosive aggressive outbursts, excessive startle responses, nightmares, flashbacks and abreactions. Reliving the trauma may even include voluntary re-enactments. A sexually abused child might become a promiscuous adult, or a physically abused child might take dangerous risks as an adult.

The second phase is the *numbing* response, characterized by emotional constriction, isolation, alienation, retreat from family obligations and the inability to experience pleasure. When you are in the numb phase, you tend to avoid any situation that might trigger a memory or an emotional outburst. Avoidance of relationships is a common experience. The phenomenological response is, "I don't feel anything. I am cold. I am just going through the motions."

The either/or, biphasic action of PTSD manifests as a fluctuation from excessive emotionality to emotional numbness with little modulation in between. You are being either overemotional or emotionally dead. You cannot modulate your responses. By fixing you in an all-or-nothing response pattern, trauma deprived you of precisely the psychological tools that you needed to cope effectively with the problems of daily living.

THE ROLE OF THE LIMBIC SYSTEM

The brain, which is divided into two halves, looks very much like a huge, gray pecan. The outer coating of the brain, commonly called gray matter, is the cerebral cortex, and it is much more developed among human beings than among the other animals. Down below the cerebral cortex, deep in the lower center of the brain where the spinal cord and the brain are joined, is the midbrain limbic system. Located here are the factory and distribution center for the brain chemicals (norepinephrine, dopamine, the catecholamines, endorphins and opioids) that control your emotions and memory.

The all-or-nothing response pattern arises from the limbic system, which performs many complex functions and contains several structures. For the purposes of this chapter, we will examine a simplified version of four limbic system structures: the hippocampus, the amygdala, the behavioral facilitation system and the behavioral inhibition system. These structures have a direct influence on how you experienced trauma and upon how you store and retrieve memory.

The Hippocampus

Bessel van der Kolk has described the *hippocampus* as a smoke detector for the brain. Constantly vigilant, it compares and contrasts all incoming data with data already in memory storage. It is concerned with the rough meaning of incoming stimuli and whether these stimuli are benign or threatening. The hippocampus serves as the librarian for memory, categorizing and storing memories it deems important. Once its screening and memory functions are complete, the hippocampus releases control of behavior.

The Amygdala

The *amygdala* governs emotions. When a threat is perceived, the amygdala determines the appropriate level of emotional response. It also organizes the sensations and emotional aspects of memory so that the hippocampus can have a total memory to store. As the BASK model shows (see Chapter 6), memory consists of behavior, affect, sensation and knowledge.

The Behavioral Facilitation And Inhibition Systems

When trauma or high stress is imminent, two related and opposing mechanisms are activated. The first is the *Behavioral Facilitating System (BFS)*, and the second is the *Behavioral Inhibiting System (BIS)*. The BFS prepares the brain for an aggressive physical response to support the amygdala's emotional response, while the BIS modulates the level of response to fit the level of threat.

When the hippocampus senses imminent trauma, it signals the amygdala and the BFS, which in turn secrete stress hormones necessary for effective action. If a total panic or rage response is indicated, the BIS remains quiet. If a modulated response is indicated, the BIS secretes enough of its specific hormones to dampen the total response down to a more acceptable level.

Think of it as grilling hamburgers. You want enough fire (BFS) to do the job; but when the fire blazes too high, the hamburgers will burn. So you spray water (BIS) on the coals to dampen the flame and keep the fire down to an appropriate level for grilling.

If the trauma is prolonged and intense, the action hormones will become depleted and the system will be unable to respond further. At that point in the trauma response, endogenous opioids, the body's natural pain-killers, will be secreted, resulting in emotional and physical numbness. (The opioid secretions have an effect roughly similar to that of a shot of heroin.) From intensity to numbness, the biochemistry of the limbic system mirrors the either/or trauma response of PTSD.

After repeated and prolonged trauma, the brain may become hypersensitive, the result being overreaction to even low levels of stress. The hippocampus increasingly loses its radar ability to screen accurately and the amygdala responds excessively to minor stresses.

When you find yourself bouncing from numbness to hyperarousal and unable to sort out your alternatives, your reasoning brain (the gray matter) must remind you that in every situation there are many options. While your emotions are saying that there are no options, your intellect can disagree. Your therapist will help you to see that there are shades of gray as well as black and white in your search for solutions.

It is important to remember that your feelings are being amplified and driven by brain chemistry. You are not crazy. It's just that your brain is repeating old functions that were required for your childhood survival, while the situation currently calls for finer, more adaptive responses in your adult life.

MEMORY

The limbic system's response to trauma also interferes with the processing of memory, which may account for some of the amnesia experienced by multiples. Sometimes an alter personality may secretly hold a complete memory for the protection of the whole personality. At other times, an alter may hold only a piece of the memory while the total memory is shared among several alters.

The hippocampus is vulnerable to stress. During times of trauma or great psychological pressure, the amygdala inhibits the hippocampus, which then cannot adequately process a memory or file it in an appropriate way. So the various parts of the memory are stored separately and randomly — behaviors, emotions, sensations and perceived meaning scattered about. Since trauma prevented these parts from being deposited together, a traumatic memory may be experienced as fragments of intense emotion, sharp bodily sensations or striking visual flashbacks without a meaningful context. Often an individual may perceive the acontextual reactions as proof of craziness, psychosomatic illness or hallucinations.

Unfortunately it is difficult to integrate these parts into a complete memory. So much fear, revulsion and shame are bound up with the memory that the system is determined not to re-experience it. At some level the whole self of the multiple "knows" what is there, even if it has been stored in fragments. All through childhood, adolescence and early adulthood, the MPD system was determined to avoid the memories. When the system finally commits to therapy as the only way out of its chaos, it will use fragmentary recollections as cues for uncovering and integrating memories. This work, of course, requires the cooperation and mutual support of the alter personalities.

Therapy will utilize your emotions or physical sensations as bridges back to where the memory was inappropriately stored. The therapist will help you search for contextual elements of the memory and will then encourage you to recollect the trauma repeatedly until the behaviors, emotions, bodily sensations and perceived meaning of the experience are assimilated and stored by the hippocampus in the correct "file." Depleted of power and processed through your frame of reference, the memory will then be available to you as needed but will no longer plague you with free-floating, intrusive emotions and strange body sensations.

It is not enough simply to uncover and abreact a traumatic experience. An unprocessed abreaction can retraumatize you unless you can meaningfully assimilate the traumatic event into a way of understanding yourself and the world. You need to remember and retell the story until it can be recited without inciting the amygdala to shut down the hippocampus. Once the memory is assimilated and filed, it should no longer have the power to torment you.

DEALING WITH YOUR RESPONSES

If you have MPD, you are aware of the psychological consequences of your disorder. You know the overwhelming emotions of terror, rage and shame. You know the confusion of having emotions and body sensations that are not linked consciously to any context. It is important to remember that your psychological experiences are paralleled by chemical processes within the limbic system of your brain.

Your excessive overreaction to both minor and major stresses is the result of your amygdala's failure to modulate your response to perceived threat. Then the awful helplessness you experience in the face of stress comes from the depletion of your action hormones; the numbness you feel is caused by naturally occurring brain opioids. Remember, your brain's response to trauma is biphasic: meltdown or shutdown.

Because the brain's response to trauma involves a neurochemical process you might think, "Surely there is a psychotropic drug that will help me." Prozac apparently helps mitigate the biphasic response of PTSD, and several drugs similar to Prozac are available. Unfortunately they appear to have mixed results with the symptoms of MPD. We can only hope that better medications in the future may provide the MPD client with enough stability to do the necessary psychotherapeutic work effectively with less pain.

Your brain's hypersensitivity may cause continued all-or-nothing responses, resulting in confusion to you and annoyance to your family and friends. If you remind yourself of your brain's disposition to see threat where there is no threat, you can use your rational mind to argue with your emotional response so that you can learn to respond in an appropriate and graduated fashion. It is not necessary to live always on the edges of panic or rage. Work with your therapist to develop strategies for dealing with your hormone-driven responses. Sometimes it helps to remember that MPD-related pain and confusion have a physiological basis.

THIRTEEN

The Devil
And Auntie

A Story by Priscilla Cogan

The following story tells of a wonderful old woman who protected children from the devil. This story is especially for child alters who survived ritual or satanic abuse. Each child in the story is given a special gift by "Auntie," and each gift provides not only a means of survival but also a way to victory over the devil. This story is meant to be read aloud.

Once upon a time,
Long, long ago
In Middle Europe,
There was a large forest.
It was called the Black Forest,
For the trees were so thick,
So tall, that the sunlight
Oft would stop
At the dense canopy of foliage
And leave the mossy ground below
Dark and unilluminated.

Being so dark and unilluminated,
The Black Forest naturally became
The place of myth and fantasy,
Of swirling images
And half-forgotten dreams,
Of ill-begotten memories,
Of wish and wisdom,
And of time lost amidst
The shadows.

In this nethershadow world,
There dwelled a group of people
Who made their living
As woodcutters —
Each owning a tiny part of the forest
Where they cut the trees
In the ancient tradition
Of coppicing.

Like their grandfathers,
And *their* grandfathers before them,
The woodcutters would seek
To clear a patch of woods
By cutting down selected hardwood,
Making sure the tree stumps
Measured two inches off the ground,
And in this cleared space
Could attract the sunlight,
So that each stump could
Give birth each year to
Shoots of new trees
Emerging out of the original tree.
In this way
The woodcutters brought the sun
Into the clearing
And watched the new offshoots
Grow from within the beginning tree.

For life begets life,
And always we are reaching
For the sun's warmth
Whether in a straight manner
Or through offshoots.
The sun nurtures us,
As love nurtures us.
Thus is the tree of life.

In this netherworld
Of deep, dense shadow
And sparse, dappled clearings,
Of misty images
And hollow sounds,
There dwelled the families
Of the woodcutters,
Who grew used to the darkness
And infrequent sun,
Who looked inside themselves
For warmth to gladden the heart,
Who knew the silence of aloneness
And the good company of the imagination
To cover hurt and heal, in part,
The lonely wound.

These were rough families,
Given to much suffering
In pursuit of their labors.
It was a hard, hard life
In the Black Forest,
And the men's and women's faces
Bore the marks and scars
Of roughness and learned hardness.
In their hearts
They knew of the Creator,
Father of Sun,
But the Devil of the cloven hoof
Was equally known
As Master of the Darkness.

Like all children in all ages,
The children of the woodcutters
Trusted in the power of their parents
And in the integrity of their parents' friends
To protect them in their innocence
From the wiles
Of the Devil of the cloven hoof,
Whose footprints could be seen,
Now and then,
On the mossy damp underground.
It was said there,
Amongst the rough and tough woodcutters,
The Devil had many friends.

Now the Devil of the cloven hoof
Likes to hurt people
And hurt them real bad,
So bad they will shun the sun
And turn to His Darkness for solace,
So bad they will hide from the light
Of truth, shamed into silence.
Hurt can do that to you . . . or me.
It can turn a person
To hate his creation
And wish for the gentle seduction
Of forgetting.
Hurt can cut as deep
As the woodcutter's axe
To the center core,
So that life must run through offshoots,
A coppicing, a coping,
A way to keep curling up toward
The diminishing sun.

Best of all, the Devil
Likes to prey upon the children
Whose faith and trust
Swell him up and

Make him High and Mighty
In the lowly underworld.

And so the Devil of the cloven hoof
Decided one day
To traipse through the Black Forest,
Stirring up trouble
Between parents and partners,
Brothers and sisters.
He built himself a lowly hut
And settled there a while. Years!

For it was the children
He was after.
A terrible spell he put them through —
Causing parents to beat their children,
Throw trust and honor out the window,
Drink to drunkenness, feign serious illness,
Make men of little heart
Prey on children of good heart,
Misusing, abusing the innocent ones.
And the forest grew darker
With the Devil's dwelling.

The children wept and stormed
And pleaded with their deaf parents
To protect them from this darkness,
And the Devil laughed at their hurt,
As their innocence was brutally ripped away
And the darkness grew and grew,
The trees blotting out the sun,
Until no one could see
What was being done to the children.

That is, except for one old woman
Called Auntie by the children.
She watched the drunken debaucheries
And the beatings of the children,
How parents and friends

Abused the innocent trust
Of the little ones.

She knew it was the Devil's doing,
And that there was little she could do,
For she was old
And at the end of her life.
Yet her heart wept at their suffering
And anger grew in her.

This old Auntie called the children of all ages
To come to her humble home, deep in the woods,
To give them each a gift,
To hold them in this time of pain
And the Devil's doing.

To the youngest child
Amongst the related group
Auntie gave white, shimmering waterwings,
Saying, "These waterwings,
My little one, will keep you buoyant,
Allow you to play and swim
As a little girl
In the stream of life
And keep that trust
That there are some good people
Out there who will not hurt you,
Who will rescue you in times of need,
But like all gifts
This gift has a price;
If you hold it too dear,
You will never learn to swim
Under your own power;
If you keep this gift too close,
You will always have the fear
The water of the forest streams
And the water of the storm
Will drown you."
Although she didn't understand the warning,

The little girl was very appreciative
Of the gift of white waterwings,
For now in all the darkness
She had found a place to play.

To the next child,
Auntie donated a translucent magnifying glass,
Saying, "My dear,
Your curiosity bubbles up inside
And seeks to explore
The world around you.
Cherish that curiosity,
But beware this, too;
When you look so close,
Make sure you can handle what you feel,
For this glass can magnify
Not just the world outside you,
But also your feelings inside,
Until all you feel is a child's rage.
Look closer still to the
Hurt inside where truth resides."
Oh, the curious child was so happy
With her new toy and set off exploring.

Next, before her stood a quiet,
Studious youngster
To whom Auntie gave a gilded book,
Saying, "Take this book
And enter a world
Of sunlight and order
And reason's reign,
Where things make sense,
Unlike the current chaos here.
But remember, too,
The mind can choke off
The chaotic feeling,
And the tight collar
Can inhibit the voice.
Do not forget to dance, my dear.

Do not forget to sing."
And very properly, the youngster
Thanked Auntie and went on her way.

The next young person strolled
Forcefully into Auntie's house,
And Auntie smiled as
She handed over the gift
Of a bejeweled sword,
Saying, "Keep this close
To remind you of your anger.
Use it to cut through
To the heart of the matter.
With this sword
You will feel strong
And have the fortitude
To do what needs to be done.
But," she cautioned,
"Don't use it to cut
Off hope and run away.
Honor your anger.
Don't let the blade grow dull
And benumbed by the evil brew and dark potions,
Lest you become like those
Who hurt you.
Be strong. For this is the sword of justice."
And the young person heard these words
And held the sword proudly by her side.

The next person at her door
Looked wounded and tired
And could not speak for all the pain
Welling up inside.
Gently, Auntie reached out
And handed her a silver pen,
Saying, "In your hand, my dear,
This pen will script your dreams
And hurts and inner song.
With this pen give life to the image.

In drawing, in the music of poetry,
Give birth to the artist
Who can fashion another world
From this netherworld you're in.
But don't let this pen
Rob your voice of the anger inside,
For that anger some day
Will give voice to you."
So smiling, the young lady departed.

Next came a young woman
Of stately presence
Upon whom Auntie bestowed
The gift of a black coat of armor,
Saying, "Nothing can hurt you now
Inside or outside.
There is no more pain,
As this coat of armor will protect you.
But remember this
When all feels dull and empty
In a world of no pain but also no joy,
Take off that armor
Briefly to feel once again."
And so this young person took
The gift, the warning, and went her way.

Next came an even older young woman
To whom Auntie
Gave the gift of a strong horse,
Saying, "Cherish this animal
That is here but
To serve a function,
To watch over you
And carry you where you dare not tread.
It is a shy, retiring horse
That will serve you well
As long as it has meaning,
For its value is in its service.
There is wisdom in this horse,

Because it knows its place
In this Creation.

Finally came the last young person,
The oldest of them all.
Auntie took pity on her
And gave her a dark blindfold
And a large yellow ball of wax,
Explaining, "To you, my dear,
I give the gift of forgetting.
The blindfold will help you
In the time of pain
So as not to see the hurt;
The wax you must put in your ears,
So as not to hear
The cry of suffering inside.
In this way you will not witness
In this hour as a child
The loss of innocence.
But be prepared, my dear,
That over the years this gift
Will make you blind and deaf
To your innermost self —
Its treasures and its hidden pain.
And there will come a time
To take off the blindfold
And unplug your ears,
To remember that which you forgot,
To redeem those parts
Of yourself
That are offshoots from the time
Of darkness and old pain."
And so she, too, gladly accepted her gift
And went on her way.

The Devil of the cloven hoof
Was not at all pleased
With how the old woman,
"That Auntie," was interfering

With his sport,
And so he sent
The Scourge of Old Age
To close her eyes in everlasting peace.
It is said that Auntie
Died with a smile on her lips,
Having outfoxed the Devil
Of his due.

For much to the Devil's surprise,
The children did not come flocking to him,
Seeking the darkness;
Rather they held strong to their gifts,
Which gave them protection
In the time of great pain.
So the Devil soon tired
After several years
And decided to move on,
Looking for less fortunate children
Who didn't have such special gifts.

You might think that his departure
Would have brought the people
Out in joy and celebration.
But, as a tree
That has been deeply axed
By the woodcutter, and
Then surprisingly spared,
Wears forever the wounded flesh,
So too the children felt their scars
And held close to their material gifts,
Not yet knowing
That the True gifts
Were the words
Of the old, kind Auntie.

A long, long time ago,
In the land of the Black Forest
And the time of the Devil's doing,

The children learned about coping
From the coppicing of the trees,
How life can circumvent the deep cut
To bring forth new life,
Offshoots, so that
The tree of life can grow
In many forms.

FOURTEEN

Cult And
Ritual Abuse

Shrouded figures, ceremonial fires, chanting, dancing, drugs, blood, sacrifice, pain, sexual defilement and death figure significantly in the memories of many clients with MPD. What to do with all this? It is a problem for both the client and the therapist.

Ritual abuse in cults is an offensive idea to most twentieth century people, mental health professionals included. Denial of repugnant or bizarre material, such as incest or cult activity, has characterized the mental health establishment's response. Despite long-held notions that reports of incest reflected the sexual desires women experienced for their fathers, incest is now recognized as real, not fantasized. However, the reality of ritual abuse continues to be denied.

Even as MPD has become a more acceptable diagnosis, the credulity of the mental health establishment is challenged again as the media showcase multiples who claim satanic abuse. The stories are just too strange, too bizarre, too "awful" to be believed.

Yet the stories do not go away. Child alters tell of being taken to the woods, to barns or to basements where animals were sacrificed and the most deranged ceremonies imaginable were practiced.

It is clear that not every cult is evil. There are cults that do not hurt children. But it is also true that some cults have used, exploited and harmed children to the extent that the children have developed multiple personalities. It is even possible that certain cults have deliberately caused the splitting of the personalities of children so that, as adults, they would return to cult leadership roles as adult alter personalities, while the host personalities carried out socially acceptable roles. Thus, a host alter might function as a respected professional person during the day, while an inner alter might serve as a satanic priest at night. Amnesic barriers enable such contradictory roles to be maintained.

One reads in the paper from time to time about religious cults that have done serious harm to children through incredible physical abuse and excessive discipline. Undoubtedly the satanic cults are the ones getting most of our attention because they have combined physical abuse with sexual abuse, drugs, pornography and an assortment of bizarre, mind-bending rituals in the worship of Satan.

A question new MPD clients ask is, "How do I know whether I have been abused by Satanists?" Some clients almost regard satanic abuse as a badge of distinction, as if it were the only "real" abuse. There can be no question about the horror of ritual abuse, but any abuse severe enough to cause a child to split is sufficiently horrible to warrant grave concern.

If you have suffered satanic or cultic abuse, it will make itself known to you. It may take longer to uncover memories of satanic abuse than others, for its victims have undoubtedly been threatened with death if they reveal cult secrets. And death was not just an implied consequence of talking; the seriousness of the threat was underscored by the child's having witnessed scenes of torture and death. Through experiential learning, the child understood the reality of the threat. Some of the cults have apparently used sophisticated brainwashing techniques to block memories and thwart therapeutic movement. Thus, cultic memories may be buried deeply and guarded fiercely.

Here are the kinds of memories that suggest ritual abuse (the first three relate to the occult but are not necessarily satanic):

- robed and hooded figures
- pentagrams and other occult symbols
- tables and/or altars with black candles
- sex involving pain, groups, animals, pictures
- mutilation and blood sacrifice, actual or simulated
- being buried alive or suspended in a dark hole or well
- being reborn as Satan's child
- being married to Satan.

Certainly, if you find ritual garments and implements in your home, they may have been used in cult ceremonies and perhaps are still being used. An internal check with all the alters may clarify the possible past and present use of such paraphernalia.

If you have memories of ritual abuse, they will surface during therapy and will be processed in the same way as are all your other traumatic experiences. It will be taken into account that a child may be so unable to accept her father as an abuser that she may perceive him as a robed monster and later, as an adult, interpret her memory as abuse by a Satanist. Not every person who has robed or candlelit memories was the victim of a cult, but many were.

The knowledgeable therapist will help you sort out your recollections and help you discover the nature of your abuse. Satanic cults have inflicted certain forms of torture on children. The person with a cultic abuse history may have recollections of certain occult symbols and rites. Each memory should be processed and respected, no matter how repugnant and "far-fetched" it appears to be.

A frightened alter who has finally gotten courage to "tell" should never be admonished that her perceptions are figments of imagination. Her "tellings" must be accepted seriously. Later, when all the memories have been processed and the system is integrated, you will have a more complete understanding of what truly happened.

FIFTEEN

Therapeutic Issues: Pitfalls And Danger Signals

Certain difficult issues and problems frequently arise during therapy. They occur so regularly among clients with MPD that it would be unusual if they did not happen to you. Being forewarned will allow you to recognize these danger signals and take appropriate steps to help yourself. Perhaps more than in any other treatment, MPD requires active teamwork between you and your therapist.

LIMITS AND BOUNDARIES

When you were a child, your abusers disregarded your boundaries and personal privacy. Such violations of your personal space complicated your developmental task of learning how to set and recognize appropriate boundaries between yourself and others. To compensate for your vulnerability to invasions of external boundaries, you developed rigid internal boundaries that isolated your alters from one another in awareness and in function.

Part of the therapeutic task is to establish appropriate and secure self-boundaries and to learn to respect the boundaries of others. Hopefully your therapist will role model this task for you by being sensitive to your needs, your strengths and your fears. He or she should also point out boundary problems in therapy as they arise. Mutual problem-solving will help you define your own personal space and identify the points at which your boundaries intersect with those of your therapist.

Your therapist will appreciate your respect for his spatial and time limits, and though your attention to these limits may be difficult, it will feel good to have someone on your side at last. For your therapist to do effective work with you and all the other clients being treated, he must have privacy and time to regroup and recenter. This means that you should phone your therapist only in times of serious crisis, when the system is absolutely unable to cope. It means that therapy will be limited to the times allotted and that sessions will begin and end at the agreed hour. Learning to operate within limits and boundaries is crucial and will encourage the alters to depend more on each other.

It is very important to be as clear as possible about your boundaries with friends, family and co-workers. Having been conditioned in childhood to invasion by others, you may discover that those around you are not respecting your limits. Learn to say no to infringements on your time and on your person.

DEPENDENCY

Dependency is a big issue. As you feel yourself becoming dependent on your therapist and the therapy hour, it may be frightening to you. After all, those upon whom you were dependent as a child were often the very ones abusing you. It is normal to feel dependent. Take the time you need to learn that in therapy you can be both dependent and safe.

Over time you will work at becoming less dependent on your therapist and develop greater mutual dependency within your own system. Each of your parts is competent in certain areas. You will find the strength, love and caring within the rich complexity of yourself that will enable you to live as a competent human being.

TRAUMATIC TRANSFERENCE

Traumatic transference will be a big problem, particularly in the early stages of therapy. Accept it as a given, and you will be able to work through it more easily.

Transference is an unavoidable way of responding to your therapist (or to anyone in a position of perceived power, for that matter). It contains all the feelings that you had for significant adults, particularly parents, when you were a child. You may feel that your therapist is just like Daddy or Mommy. This will be especially true during times of emotional intensity in therapy.

If Daddy was an abuser, you may occasionally perceive your male therapist as an abuser. Some of your parts will swear to it and beg you not to trust or be vulnerable to him. Be grateful for having at least one inner personality who is suspicious and careful. You have probably been saved from bad situations in the past because of that inner warning. Of course, you must keep reminding all your parts that your therapist is not your Daddy and that the times of abuse are long past.

You may find yourself setting up litmus tests for your therapist, tests that cannot be passed. "Do you remember what you said on August 16, 1990? Oh, you don't? Obviously you don't care about us very much." Your therapist may be able to clarify what is happening in a way that everyone can accept with good humor.

Traumatic transference *will happen* in therapy, and it can be used in a positive way leading to growth. The particular alter involved and the therapist should discuss the transference with reference to its origins and take note that the childhood abuse is no longer occurring. Therapy takes place not only in a different time and space from the abuse situation but also in a safe environment. The time of abuse and danger is past. More important, you learn through the discussion of transference that you are in control this time, not the abuser.

You must also know a sad truth. There are unethical therapists who have misused and abused their clients. A wary alter can sound a crucial warning if the therapy is becoming inappropriate. You have to discern between those alters who are overly cautious and those who are rightfully worried.

RUNNING FROM THERAPY

Even if everything is proceeding in treatment, there will be times you may panic and want to run from therapy. You will hear the plea, "Get us out of here!" Alters can provide amazingly creative reasons for leaving therapy. You will be surprised, but do not be taken off guard.

Usually this happens because some of the alters fear that secrets are about to be exposed. Keeping secrets was your path to survival as a child. Only through mastery and cooperation within the system will you be able to work through hidden memories effectively. Even then some of your alters will experience great fear over what may be exposed.

Sometimes leaving therapy is caused by external factors, such as job or insurance loss. Many MPD clients have experienced so much chaos in their lives that they live in financial ruin. Do everything possible to maintain financial stability, and cover yourself through the end of your therapy.

Accept the fact that the desire to quit therapy will happen from time to time. Accept the legitimate motivations behind the desire, but remember that *only those who successfully complete therapy will ever emerge from the terror, chaos and shame they have lived in since childhood.*

REMAINING IN ABUSIVE SITUATIONS

It sometimes happens that an adult client continues to live in the parental home and is still being abused. If this is your situation, it is important that your dissociative defenses remain intact, for they are your best survival mechanisms. Instead your therapist will do supportive work and crisis management with you. Only after you have escaped your abusive environment and are living independently can the full MPD treatment process begin.

RELIVING ABUSIVE SITUATIONS

Some MPD clients find themselves in abusive situations over and over again. Though not the same as their childhood situations, the new ones recapitulate their experience of being abused, hurt, manipulated and humiliated and also feed their shame.

Individuals with MPD are not the only ones who follow such a path. You probably know someone raised in an alcoholic environment who grew up to marry an alcoholic. Quite often such people adopt the same marital roles they played in their families of origin. We all tend to repeat that which is familiar to us, even if it is unhealthy.

If you have repeatedly found yourself in abusive relationships, think about how it happened. Do you recognize the danger signals? Your therapy will help you become more alert to these signals so that you can prevent your revictimization. If others are repeatedly taking advantage of you and hurting you, develop strategies to either change the situation or get out of it.

CONTINUOUS ABREACTIONS

The experience of continuous abreactions may be what brought you to therapy. You have heard that abreacting traumatic memories is the only way to get peace, and it may be confusing when your therapist initially discourages the practice. Continuous abreactions are neither desirable nor therapeutic. The most important part of therapy is to develop strength and cooperation among all your parts. You must develop mastery within your system before effective abreactions can be accomplished. If all of your psychic energy is spent suffering through bits and pieces of traumatic memories, you will have little left for your therapy, family, friends or job.

You and your therapist working together must help all your parts develop mastery of anxiety and save the memory work until it is appropriate. This is not as dramatic as continued abreactions and you do not have the temporary release of an uncompleted abreaction, but it will avoid continual chaos, destabilization and inability to function.

SELF-HARM

Thoughts of self-harm are probably not new to you. Under extreme abuse an alter may be created who can identify with the abusers and, by joining them, be able to predict potential abuse and thereby avoid it, mitigate its severity or redirect it, thus preserving the self from additional pain or terror. Known as the Stockholm Syndrome, it has been observed in many hostage situations. It is one way a personality may deal with inescapable terror.

However, if you experience bouts of self-harm, it is not necessarily an identification with the abuser. Quite often it is a way to "wake up," to come alive. An individual who is in terror may shut down all feelings, in effect becoming dead to emotions and sensations. When one is exhausted by terror, numbness may seem the only way to cope. Yet feeling dead is frightening too; so the individual may cut or otherwise hurt the body as a way of forcing it to feel again. Therapists often hear the statement, "I feel most alive when I cut myself."

To an outside observer, the individual oscillating from agitation to depression to self-harm may seem to be trying to manipulate family and friends for some selfish gain. But the outside observer fails to understand what is really happening: an alter is either trying to punish the body on behalf of the abusers, or it is trying to awaken the body from its living death.

As therapy progresses the alters will find more direct and effective ways of expressing anger, modulating terror and breaking through the numbness. They will come to disavow the pain and torture inflicted upon them by their childhood abusers and will learn to value the body as the vehicle of expression for all the alter personalities.

SUBSTANCE ABUSE

If you have MPD, the chances are great that you have abused drugs and alcohol and may still be doing so. These substances may mimic the self-soothing release of your own internal opioids. The problem of self-medication with alcohol or drugs is that it can work only temporarily and will impede your recovery. If you are being anesthetized by alcohol or drugs, your feelings are not available for therapy. All parts of your mind must be clear for the work to succeed.

ESCAPE FROM RESPONSIBILITY

It is important that you fulfill the duties of everyday life such as holding a job, caring for yourself and your family, cleaning house or doing any of those things you expect from yourself. MPD should not be an excuse for irresponsibility. Life goes on, and responsibilities continue. With proper therapy and your own strong commitment, you should be able to take care of yourself and your obligations, complete therapy and look toward the future.

A FINAL WORD

MPD therapy is a long, hard, arduous process for you and your therapist. It demands diligent work to develop the capacities and resources of all your self parts. It will enlist all those capacities and resources to recover and process your hidden memories. Finally, it will require the incorporation of your alter parts into a new and whole person. There is probably no other therapy in which your commitment and diligence is so necessary. Fortunately the prognosis is excellent if you have a competent therapist and you are ready to work hard. Do the work, become whole, and no one inside will be lost or dismissed.

*LET THE JOURNEY INTO
WHOLENESS BEGIN.*

RESOURCES

The following two booklets are for individuals with MPD. They contain some of the same material as is found in *The Fractured Mirror: Multiple Personality Disorder*, but with a slightly different slant:

Branscomb, Louisa. *Becoming Whole: Dissociation And Me*. Decatur, GA: Lodestar Productions, 1990.

Gil, Eliana. *United We Stand: A Book For People With Multiple Personalities*. Walnut Creek, CA: Launch Press, 1990.

The next book is written, in part, by professional therapists, but the majority is written by individuals being treated for MPD. It is an excellent resource.

Cohen, Giller and W. *Multiple Personality Disorder From The Inside Out*. Baltimore, MD: Sidran Press, 1991.

The following two books are for therapists and may be more technical than you want, but they are excellent. Putnam's book is the standard work in the field; it is rich in information and very technical. Ross's book may be more readable for a layperson.

Putnam, Frank. *Diagnosis and Treatment of Multiple Personality Disorder.* New York: Guilford Press, 1989.

Ross, Colin. *Multiple Personality Disorder: Diagnosis, Clinical Features, and Treatment.* New York: John Wiley & Sons, 1989.

The following books, while not written specifically for survivors with MPD, contain very useful information and guidance.

Bass, Ellen and Laura Davis. *The Courage To Heal.* New York: Harper & Row, 1988.

Graber, Ken. *Ghosts In The Bedroom.* Deerfield Beach, FL: Health Communications, 1991.

Forward, Susan. *Toxic Parents.* New York: Bantam Books, 1989.

Many Voices is a wonderful newsletter for people with MPD. I recommend it to all my clients, and I read it regularly myself. It is worth the subscription.

Many Voices: Words Of Hope For People With MPD Or A Dissociative Disorder. Published bimonthly, P.O. Box 2639, Cincinnati, OH 45201-2639.

BIBLIOGRAPHY

Bliss, E. L. Multiple personalities. A report of 14 cases with implications for schizophrenia. *Archives of General Psychiatry* 37 (1980): 1388-97.

Bradshaw, John. *Healing The Shame That Binds You.* Deerfield Beach, FL: Health Communications, 1988.

Braun, B. G. The BASK Model Of Dissociation. *Dissociation* 1 (1988): 4-23.

Chu, James. The critical issues task force report: the role of hypnosis and amytal interviews in the recovery of traumatic memories. *ISSMP&D News* 10 (1992): 6-9.

Crabtree, Adam. *Multiple Man.* Westport, CT: Praeger Publishers, 1985.

Diagnostic And Statistical Manual of Mental Disorders, 3d ed. rev. Washington, D.C.: American Psychiatric Association, 1987.

Ellenberger, H. *The Discovery Of The Unconscious.* New York: Basic Books, 1970.

Greaves, G. B. Multiple personality 165 years after Mary Reynolds. *Journal of Nervous and Mental Disease* 168 (1980): 577-96.

Keyes., D. *The Minds Of Billy Milligan.* New York: Random House, 1981.

Kluft, Richard. Making the diagnosis of multiple personality disorder (MPD). *Directions In Psychiatry* 5: Lesson 23.

Lowenstein, Richard, ed. Multiple Personality Disorder. *The Psychiatric Clinics Of North America* 14 (1991).

Mellody, Pia. *Shame: Legacy Of Abuse, Gift Of God* (cassette tape). Wickenberg, AZ: Mellody Enterprises, 1989.

Montgomery, J. W., ed. *Demon Possession*. Minneapolis: Bethany House, 1976.

Nathanson, Donald. *Shame And Pride*. New York: W. W. Norton, 1992.

Papousek, H., and M. Papousek. Cognitive aspects of preverbal social interaction between human infants and adults. *Parent Infant Interaction*. New York: Association of Scientific Publications, 1975.

Putnam, Frank. Evoked potentials in multiple personality disorder. Presented at American Psychiatric Association, 1982.

Ross, Colin. *Multiple Personality Disorder: Diagnosis, Clinical Features, and Treatment*. New York: John Wiley & Sons, 1989.

Ross, Colin. "Theory of Multiplicity." Fourth Annual Eastern Regional Conference on Abuse and Multiple Personality, Alexandria, VA, 1992.

Ross, Colin; Lynne Ryan; Harrison Voigt; and Kyle Eide. High and low dissociators in a college student population. *Dissociation* 4 (1991).

Schreiber, F. R. *Sybil*. Chicago: Henry Regnery, 1973.

Sizemore, C., and E. Pettillo. *I'm Eve*. New York: Doubleday, 1977.

Thigpen, C. H., and H. M. Cleckley. *The Three Faces of Eve*. New York: McGraw-Hill, 1957.

Tomkins, Silvan. *Affect/Imagery/Consciousness: The Positive Affects*, Vol. 1. New York: Springer, 1962.

Tomkins, Silvan. *Affect/Imagery/Consciousness: The Negative Affects*, Vol 2. New York: Springer, 1963.

Tomkins, Silvan. *Affect/Imagery/Consciousness: The Negative Affects: Anger and Fear,* Vol 3. New York: Springer, 1991.

van der Kolk, Bessel. *Psychological Trauma.* Washington, D.C.: American Psychiatric Press, 1987.

van der Kolk, Bessel. The trauma spectrum: the interaction of biological and social events in the genesis of the trauma response. *Journal Of Traumatic Stress* 1 (1988).

van der Kolk, Bessel, and Jose Saporta. The biological response to psychic trauma: mechanisms and treatment of intrusion and numbing. *Anxiety Research* 4 (1991a).

van der Kolk, Bessel; Christopher Perry; and Judith Herman. Childhood origins of self-destructive behavior. *American Journal Of Psychiatry* 148 (1991b).

Watkins, J. G., ed. *The Therapeutic Self.* New York: Human Sciences Press, 1978.

INDEX